Modern furnishings
in the lobby
library of New York
City's Nolitan.

THE WORLD'S GREATEST
HOTELS

2012 EDITION

THE WORLD'S GREATEST
HOTELS

2012 EDITION

TRAVEL+
LEISURE
BOOKS

AMERICAN EXPRESS PUBLISHING CORPORATION
NEW YORK

TRAVEL + LEISURE
THE WORLD'S GREATEST HOTELS
SEVENTH EDITION

Editor Jennifer Miranda
Consulting Editors Laura Begley Bloom, Irene Edwards
Art Director Phoebe Flynn Rich
Consulting Art Director Wendy Scofield
Photo Editor Beth Garrabrant
Production Associate David Richey
Editorial Assistant Lindsey Olander
Reporters Rebecca Dalzell, James Jung, Jane Margolies, Kathryn O'Shea-Evans
Copy Editors David Gunderson, Mike Iveson, Sarah Khan, Libby Sentz
Researchers Joseph Harper, Charles Moore, Paola Singer

TRAVEL + LEISURE
Editor-in-Chief Nancy Novogrod
Design Director Sandra Garcia
Executive Editor Jennifer Barr
Managing Editor Laura Teusink
Arts/Research Editor Mario R. Mercado
Copy Chief Kathy Roberson
Photo Editor Whitney Lawson
Production Manager Ayad Sinawi

AMERICAN EXPRESS PUBLISHING CORPORATION
President and Chief Executive Officer Ed Kelly
Chief Marketing Officer and President, Digital Media
Mark V. Stanich
CFO, SVP, Corporate Development and Operations
Paul B. Francis
VP, General Managers Frank Bland, Keith Strohmeier
VP, Books and Products Marshall Corey
Director, Books Programs Bruce Spanier
Senior Marketing Manager, Branded Books Eric Lucie
Assistant Marketing Manager Stacy Mallis
Director of Fulfillment and Premium Value
Philip Black
Manager of Customer Experience and Product Development Charles Graver
Director of Finance Thomas Noonan
Associate Business Manager Uma Mahabir
Operations Director Anthony White

Cover: Dusk at Aman Sveti Stefan's Villa Miločer, in Montenegro.
Photographed by Malú Alvarez

ISBN 978-1-932624-44-1

Published by American Express
Publishing Corporation
1120 Avenue of the Americas
New York, New York 10036

Distributed by Charlesbridge Publishing
85 Main Street, Watertown, Massachusetts 02472

Printed in Canada

The terrace lounge off La Banane's Juliette Deluxe Bungalow, in Baie de Lorient, St. Bart's.

Cabanas lining the teak pool deck at Mr. C Beverly Hills, in Los Angeles.

CONTENTS

contents

7

KEY TO THE PRICE ICONS $ UNDER $250 $$ $250–$499 $$$ $500–$749 $$$$ $750–$999 $$$$$ $1,000 AND UP

Neo-Gothic details
in London's St. Pancras
Renaissance Hotel.

contents

9

KEY TO THE PRICE ICONS $ UNDER $250 $$ $250–$499 $$$ $500–$749 $$$$ $750–$999 $$$$$ $1,000 AND UP

A brace of resident ducks at an entrance to Babylonstoren's farm, in South Africa.

KEY TO THE PRICE ICONS $ UNDER $250 $$ $250–$499 $$$ $500–$749 $$$$ $750–$999 $$$$$ $1,000 AND UP

The reception
desk at the
Corinthia Hotel,
in London.

INTRODUCTION

I approach hotel rooms gingerly—a behavior that has become more pronounced, rather than reduced, by the frequency with which I travel. I don't bring along scented candles, family photos, or other domestic talismans to sprinkle around the surfaces. I don't expend effort trying to make my hotel room feel like home. What's the use?

The point of being in a hotel is the pleasure of *not* being at home—eating breakfast delivered by room service; having someone to worry about your comfort level or complain to when it's not met. The hotels I especially love make some reference to their region, whether subtle or unmistakable. Surrendering to a kind of floating sense of otherness, of just passing through, I have found, is often the best way to experience a destination.

The trick is to find lodgings that invite you to both kick back and dive in. In light of this, we give you *Travel + Leisure*'s seventh edition of *The World's Greatest Hotels,* our editors' selection of the year's best places to stay. From the Dorothy Draper–designed florals of West Virginia's resurrected Greenbrier resort to the concrete walls and skyline views of Shanghai's Waterhouse at South Bund, these properties shine a light on what T+L readers have always sought: larger-than-life exploits and a soft landing in which to enjoy them.

It should come as no surprise that this volume is populated by discoveries in remote and exotic destinations—clear confirmation that exploration, adventure, and authenticity have become the holy trinity for today's inveterate travelers. The hawker market at Six Senses Con Dao, located in a little-known archipelago off

Vietnam, offers the type of immersive encounter our readers treasure, as does Singita Explore, a mobile safari camp in sight of zebras and antelope in Tanzania's Grumeti Reserve.

This is not to say that familiar locales do not afford similarly life-enriching opportunities. There are few more diverting joys than wandering the streets of an up-and-coming neighborhood, one of the activities New York City's quirky Nolitan encourages you to savor. The St. Regis Florence, in a 15th-century palazzo originally designed by Filippo Brunelleschi, tempts you to linger on the past. Even a classic resort town takes on new appeal at Hotel Encanto, a minimalist compound overlooking Acapulco.

Though much of our sourcing has been internal—that is, from our editors' favorite stories published in our magazine—the back of this book features input from T+L readers in the World's Best Awards and the T+L 500, tried-and-true guides to the globe's top spots, where you'll find ultra-luxe safari sites, sleek skyscraper hotels, and rustic countryside inns. Beyond that, there's an index and directory to help you search for properties by location and category, from family-friendly to affordable. After all, ensuring your travels are as feasible, interesting, and memorable as they can be is our mission.

NANCY NOVOGROD EDITOR-IN-CHIEF

Custom bikes parked at the entrance to Ruschmeyer's, in Montauk, New York.

MAINERHODEISLANDNEWYORKNEWYORKCITYWESTVIR
MONTANAWYOMINGCOLORADOPARKCITYOREGONLOSANG

UNITED STATES
+CANADA

NIACHARLESTONFLORIDAMIAMICHICAGOSANANTONIO
ESKAUAIOAHUNEWFOUNDLANDBRITISHCOLUMBIAMAINE

KENNEBUNKPORT, MAINE

TIDES BEACH CLUB

CAST AWAY ANY PRECONCEIVED NOTIONS of a stuffy New England grande dame. In this bastion of the East Coast preppy set, the Tides Beach Club puts a fresh spin on a classic summer retreat. The restoration of the 1899 Victorian preserves the wraparound porch and rocking chairs but opts for clean lines and muted sea colors in the 21 guest rooms. (Two suites come outfitted with brightly printed rugs and geometric headboards, courtesy of style guru Jonathan Adler.) Birch-lined country paths beckon for exploration; on sunny days, the hotel's designated "beach tenders" roll out towels along neighboring Goose Rocks Beach. Come nightfall, a bonfire blazes five minutes away at sister resort Hidden Pond, encouraging guests to swap stories beneath the stars.

254 Kings Hwy.; 207/967-3757; tidesbeachclubmaine.com; doubles from $$.

A view of the Tides Beach Club at sunset.

Goose Rocks Beach. Above: One of two suites designed by Jonathan Adler.

A lantern-lit walkway on the grounds of Forty 1° North. Below: Playing pool in the library.

NEWPORT, RHODE ISLAND

FORTY 1° NORTH

AT THE TURN OF THE 20TH CENTURY, society figures with names like Astor and Vanderbilt made Newport a coastal haven synonymous with Gilded Age glamour. Now the LEED-certified Forty 1° North blends that storied legacy with eco-conscious credibility and a contemporary design sensibility. On a prime marina-side location at—you guessed it—latitude 41 north, the white-shingled structure contains multiple references to the life aquatic, from shimmering tile backsplashes to a sand-and-sea-inspired color palette in the public spaces. A massive wooden chess set reinforces the playful spirit, as do the wicker swings and retro swimwear mural at the casual dockside restaurant, Christie's. Arriving by yacht? The hotel's deckhands are standing by to tie you ashore.

351 Thames St.; 401/846-8018; 41north.com; doubles from $$.

Enjoying cocktails
at the Grill
restaurant's outdoor
seating area.

The Bedford Post Inn's farmhouse-style exterior.

BEDFORD POST INN

WHEN ACTORS RICHARD GERE AND CAREY LOWELL decided to try their hand at the hotel business, some might have expected a flashy property fit for the Hollywood Hills. Instead, the couple—longtime residents of New York's Westchester County—set their sights on a dilapidated Dutch-colonial house built on a tangle of Revolutionary War–era riding trails, transforming it into an eight-room inn with all the trappings of a country estate. Lowell helped design the understated rooms, most of which feature working fireplaces and soaking tubs handcrafted in Portugal. An airy yoga loft with burnished wood floors is the place for morning sun salutations before a brisk walk through the woodlands. House-baked goods at the Barn café hit the spot afterward. Meanwhile, the seasonally driven restaurant, Farmhouse, has become the talk of the town, expertly turning out *hamachi crudo,* egg-filled ravioli, and a strip loin with charred ramps and bone-marrow toast. And yes, that's Martha Stewart sitting in the corner.

954 Old Post Rd.; 914/205-3773; bedfordpostinn.com; doubles from $$.

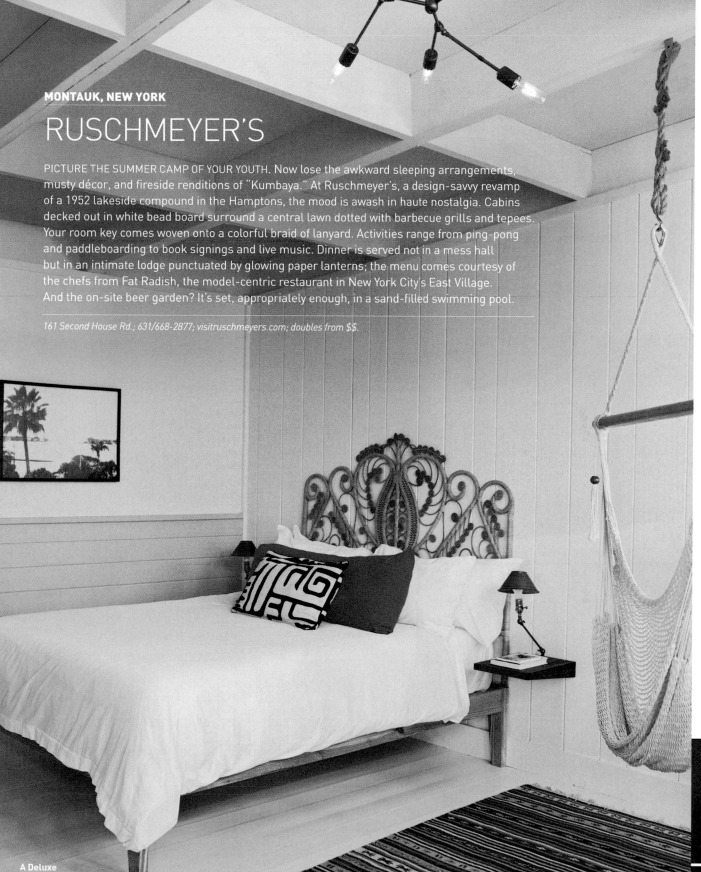

RUSCHMEYER'S

PICTURE THE SUMMER CAMP OF YOUR YOUTH. Now lose the awkward sleeping arrangements, musty décor, and fireside renditions of "Kumbaya." At Ruschmeyer's, a design-savvy revamp of a 1952 lakeside compound in the Hamptons, the mood is awash in haute nostalgia. Cabins decked out in white bead board surround a central lawn dotted with barbecue grills and tepees. Your room key comes woven onto a colorful braid of lanyard. Activities range from ping-pong and paddleboarding to book signings and live music. Dinner is served not in a mess hall but in an intimate lodge punctuated by glowing paper lanterns; the menu comes courtesy of the chefs from Fat Radish, the model-centric restaurant in New York City's East Village. And the on-site beer garden? It's set, appropriately enough, in a sand-filled swimming pool.

161 Second House Rd.; 631/668-2877; visitruschmeyers.com; doubles from $$.

A Deluxe
queen room at
Ruschmeyer's.

NEW YORK CITY

WHEN WAS GOTHAM'S GOLDEN AGE? If the city's latest hotel openings are any indication, there are more answers to that question than you might expect. Here, you'll find your favorite iteration of Manhattan—from the glamorously roaring to the understatedly modern.

1 THE CHATWAL

A hangout in the 1930's for the likes of Fred Astaire, Irving Berlin, and John Barrymore, midtown's Lambs Club has been reinvented as the 76-room Chatwal, with designer Deco touches (red-leather banquettes; terrazzo floors; wood paneling) by Thierry Despont. In keeping with the theme, bellhops wear pillbox hats at the check-in desk and rooms are stocked with backgammon sets and copies of *The Great Gatsby*.

ROOM TO BOOK Deluxe guest rooms have suede-covered walls, leather-wrapped closets, and our favorite: many have French doors that lead to a spacious private terrace with a heated floor. **DON'T MISS** Downstairs, the bar at the appropriately named Lambs Club restaurant turns out retro cocktails by Milk & Honey mixologist Sasha Petraske, who pioneered the city's speakeasy trend.

130 W. 44th St.; 800/325-3589 or 212/764-6200; thechatwalny.com; doubles from $$$$.

Mezzanine Bar at the Chatwal.

2 HÔTEL AMERICANO

Touches of Midcentury Modern embellish the rooms and public spaces at Hôtel Americano, in the burgeoning West Chelsea art gallery district. The first U.S. outpost of the Mexican chain Grupo Habita is furnished with 1960's beanbag chairs from Milan, wood-paneled sleeping platforms, and built-in desks topped with push-button phones and analog alarm clocks. **ROOM TO BOOK** Uptown Studio suites come with marble baths featuring deep soaking tubs and Aēsop products, and mod chrome hanging fireplaces. **DON'T MISS** Nightlife connoisseurs flock to the Americano's two subterranean bars, which resemble upscale Atomic Age bunkers. A glass elevator that runs along the building's exterior transports everyone to the rooftop pool, which becomes a hot tub in winter.

518 W. 27th St.; 212/216-0000; hotel-americano.com; doubles from $$.

3 TRUMP SOHO

Forget such over-the-top Trump signatures as gold banisters and floor-to-ceiling marble: in SoHo, the color scheme is muted and the vibe contemporary. To that end, headboards are puckered Fendi leather, sheets are custom-made Bellino, and views span from the Hudson River straight to the Verrazano Bridge. **ROOM TO BOOK** The largest of the hotel's Trump SoHo Spa suites has a two-person sauna, a shower outfitted with soothing hydrotherapy jets, and direct access to a private treatment room in the 11,000-square-foot complex. **DON'T MISS** The bi-level, mosaic-tiled day spa is home to NYC's first luxury Turkish hammam, inspired by Ivanka Trump's travels in Istanbul. Also on offer: a seventh-floor alfresco pool deck.

246 Spring St.; 877/828-7080 or 212/842-5500; trumpsohohotel.com; doubles from $$$.

One of Hôtel Americano's Uptown Studio suites.

Trump SoHo's neutral-toned lobby.

4 THE JAMES

The atmosphere at SoHo's James hotel is that of a stylishly pared-down bachelor pad, thanks to masculine reclaimed-wood floors, floor-to-ceiling windows, and glass-enclosed bathrooms that lend an air of sexiness. Subtle artwork (a mosaic made of used computer keys in an elevator lobby; inlaid glass walls in an elevator) appears throughout. **ROOM TO BOOK** A Corner King Studio suite is marked by two walls of windows that have expansive city vistas. Custom furniture and natural linens complete the look. **DON'T MISS** The multilevel Urban Garden houses a restaurant by David Burke, a pop-up farmers' market, and a site for outdoor film screenings. At the top-floor pool area, a tanning concierge ensures the perfect glow, instructing you when to turn over via text message.

27 Grand St.; 888/526-3778 or 212/465-2000; jameshotels.com; doubles from $$.

City views from the James's rooftop pool.

5 MONDRIAN SOHO

Another equally anticipated arrival channels a moody kind of glamour inspired by Jean Cocteau's 1946 film *La Belle et la Bête*. Bold blue accents (vine-patterned throw pillows; plush, wall-to-wall carpeting; sumptuous sofas in the lobby) offset slick chrome fixtures and delicate details such as antique sconces and Beaux-Arts chandeliers. **ROOM TO BOOK** A picture window behind the bed in north-facing room No. 2303 captures midtown Manhattan's evening skyline to brilliant effect. **DON'T MISS** For an experience on par with dining in a greenhouse, head to the glass-roofed Imperial No. Nine. The sustainable seafood restaurant sets the tone with wrought-iron garden furniture, verdant potted plants and ficus trees, and chandeliers dripping with crystals.

9 Crosby St.; 800/606-6090 or 212/389-1000; mondriansoho.com; doubles from $$.

6 THE NOLITAN

The first boutique hotel in the area north of Little Italy, the Nolitan reflects the neighborhood's quirky zeitgeist with a fleet of skateboards for exploring the shop-lined streets nearby and personalized organic grocery shopping to fill your mini fridge. Pets are pampered just as attentively as the guests: dogs get toys and treats during your stay. **ROOM TO BOOK** You can see the Williamsburg Bridge bathed in morning sunlight from your bed in suite No. 802; the Empire State Building is best eyed during a soak in the bathroom's spacious freestanding tub. **DON'T MISS** Ellabess, an oak and Carrara marble dining room on the hotel's ground floor, serves up seasonal American favorites such as fried chicken with pickled watermelon rind and peeky-toe crab salad with squash and *uni* butter.

30 Kenmare St.; 877/665-4826 or 212/925-2555; nolitanhotel.com; doubles from $$.

A penthouse perch in the Mondrian SoHo.

A light-filled corner of the lobby at the Nolitan.

The corridor outside the Crystal Ballroom at the Greenbrier.

THE GREENBRIER

THE LEGENDARY DOROTHY DRAPER—she of the cabbage-rose patterns and baroque plaster moldings—ruled the world of interior design for a large part of the 20th century. And the Greenbrier, a 6,750-acre enclave in the Allegheny Mountains, was the improbable jewel in her crown. After an extensive renovation, the Draper touch is still very much in evidence: resort curator Carleton Varney, her protégé, keeps a vast inventory of Draper's fabric designs in circulation, and periodically leads weeklong decorating workshops. The famous falconry course remains, as does the guided tour through a Cold War–era bunker. Admittedly, a few of the changes (a casino; a steak house where Wagyu beef is ordered by the ounce) have raised some eyebrows among the Greenbrier's old guard. But surely even Draper would have approved of the restored 1950's Pullman cars that will soon be available to transport guests directly from Washington, D.C.

300 W. Main St.; 800/624-6070 or 304/536-1110; greenbrier.com; doubles from $$.

The hotel's indoor swimming pool.

The Grand Mansion Suite
at Wentworth Mansion.

The hotel's rooftop cupola. Right: Antelope au poivre, served at Circa 1886 restaurant.

WENTWORTH MANSION

IN THE SOUTH, HOSPITALITY ISN'T JUST A TRADITION; it's a deeply ingrained way of life. The atmosphere is as genteel as you'd expect at the Wentworth Mansion, a cotton magnate's former residence in the center of Charleston's historic district. No detail was overlooked in the 1886 main house, from the hand-carved marble mantels to the Tiffany stained-glass panels. The 21 rooms come with king-size sleigh beds and whirlpool tubs. A rooftop cupola provides panoramic views of the city. And in the onetime carriage house, whose wooden stable doors and heart-pine floors remain intact, the restaurant Circa 1886 puts a modern spin on Lowcountry fare. Retreat into one of the intimate booths, designed to mimic the original carriage stalls, to enjoy roast chicken and Carolina trout the way they did in the old days: by candlelight.

149 Wentworth St.; 888/466-1886 or 843/853-1886; wentworthmansion.com; doubles from $$.

VERO BEACH, FLORIDA

COSTA D'ESTE BEACH RESORT

HOMETOWN HERO GLORIA ESTEFAN—beloved in these parts for much more than her multiplatinum music career—continues to buck the celebrity-hotelier curse with her second endeavor in the Sunshine State. The singer and her husband, Emilio, own the Costa d'Este Beach Resort, a slice of Rat Pack–style swagger on Vero Beach, 2½ hours north of Miami. Art Deco–inspired touches such as built-in portholes and sinuous walls create a timeless south Florida look; Midcentury nods include teak wall paneling and mod, bubble-themed wallpaper. Palm trees sway on the ocean-facing pool deck, where the chaises are made for two and the tunes come straight from Gloria's personal iPod. On weekends, a DJ spins live for the town's burgeoning up-all-night crowd. A nightly mojito hour serves as a tribute to the Estefans' Cuban heritage.

3244 Ocean Dr.; 877/562-9919 or 772/562-9919; costadeste.com; doubles from $$.

HOTEL
BEAUX ARTS

YOU DON'T NEED LEBRON JAMES to tell you that downtown Miami is heating up. For proof, check in to the 44-room Hotel Beaux Arts Miami, a hotel-within-a-hotel on floors 38 through 40 of the JW Marriott Marquis. Amenities are worthy of a basketball superstar—extra-long beds; 55-inch flat-screen TV's—and there's an NBA-approved court on site, along with a virtual bowling alley and a high-definition indoor golf simulator. The dazzle continues at DB Bistro Moderne, the first Miami outpost from Daniel Boulud, where the signature item is a braised short-rib burger topped with foie gras and truffles. And in a city whose cultural offerings just keep getting better, the hotel is down the block from the $465 million Adrienne Arsht Center for the Performing Arts. For the hottest ticket in town, however, head to the nearby American Airlines Arena and get a live-action look at LeBron himself.

255 Biscayne Blvd. Way; 888/717-8858 or 305/421-8702; marriott.com; doubles from $$.

L'Atelier, the lounge on Hotel Beaux Arts Miami's 39th floor.

united states + canada

31

A sunbathing spot stocked with chilled drinks along the shore at Soho Beach House.

SOHO BEACH HOUSE

FOR A HOSPITALITY GROUP that has staked its name on exclusivity, the Soho Beach House is surprisingly welcoming. The latest incarnation of the U.K.-based social club is set well away from the South Beach scene, with a cozy, denlike atmosphere that brings to mind Latin America by way of London. Guest rooms feature terrazzo floors and tropical furnishings; a Cuban coffee bar stocked with rare cigars lies just off a drawing room with ye-olde-club chairs and an art collection curated by prominent critic Francesca Gavin. Cecconi's, the Mayfair hot spot, has a branch here, serving Venetian specialties in a garden courtyard amid trees gilded in lights. And the menu at Cowshed spa, a favorite with the aristo set, combines otherworldly indulgence with a dose of British humor; case in point: the relaxing Knackered Cow massage.

4385 Collins Ave.; 786/507-7900; sohobeachhouse. com; doubles from $$.

united states + canada

A bellman in uniform at the entrance to Public Chicago.

CHICAGO

PUBLIC

"I DON'T THINK LUXURY is based on what you pay for something," Ian Schrager says. "It's about an experience." And at the Public Chicago, that experience is decidedly democratic, a surprise from the man who practically created the velvet-rope concept. Collaborating with his long-term design staff and Yabu Pushelberg, Schrager transformed the former Ambassador East hotel into his most personal project yet. Instead of three-legged seating by Philippe Starck, there are linen-covered armchairs based on a Paris flea market find. A series of cow photographs by Jean-Baptiste Mondino winks at Chicago's famous meat market. The Pump Room, the hotel's original restaurant and a former hangout of Humphrey Bogart and Marilyn Monroe, now serves the winning small plates of Jean-Georges Vongerichten's ABC Kitchen. As if to underscore Schrager's new philosophy, room service arrives not on a silver tray but in a brown paper bag—and tastes no less delicious for it.

1301 N. State Pkwy.; 888/506-3471 or 312/787-3700; publichotels.com; doubles from $.

Incandescent orbs hanging in the Pump Room restaurant. Above: The hotel's Living Room.

The library at Hotel Havana. Left: The hotel's Mediterranean-inspired façade.

SAN ANTONIO, TEXAS

HOTEL HAVANA

THE ICONOCLASTIC LIZ LAMBERT helped jump-start South Austin's bohemian resurgence when she turned an old motor court into the funky Hotel San José. Then came Hotel Saint Cecilia, a few blocks away, and her chic trailer park at El Cosmico, in the West Texas art colony of Marfa. Now Lambert has come to San Antonio, converting a 1914 Mediterranean Revival building on a wooded stretch of the Riverwalk district known as Museum Reach. At the Hotel Havana, tufted-velvet recamiers, wrought-iron headboards, and dark Bastrop-pine floors evoke a Spanish-colonial feel, enhanced by the flickering glow of votives in the subterranean lounge. The Latin American menu at Ocho includes fresh-fried churros for breakfast and a traditional pozole for lunch and dinner, complemented by a drinks list that showcases tequilas, rums, and mescals. Lambert doesn't appear to be losing her Midas touch: Hotel Havana, like her previous properties, has become *the* place to see and be seen.

1015 Navarro St.; 210/222-2008; havanasanantonio.com; doubles from $.

The dark-wood
staircase
in the lobby.

One of the luxurious tents at the Resort at Paws Up.

GREENOUGH, MONTANA

RESORT AT PAWS UP

SEVEN YEARS AGO, WHEN THE RESORT AT PAWS UP first came upon the scene, "glamping" was a relatively exotic concept. Now it's an industry trend. The juxtaposition of rough-and-tumble wilderness and posh creature comforts appeals to adventurers and romantics alike—and Paws Up continues to lead the pack with its recently opened Pinnacle Camp, an enclave of six tents on a ridge overlooking Elk Creek and the Blackfoot River. John Wayne types might scoff at the jetted tubs and Oriental rugs, but the surrounding scenery is as rugged and authentic as it gets. Elk and white-tailed deer gambol through the forest of lodgepole pines; owls hoot from their perches high in the Douglas firs. As at any mountain retreat, guests have prime access to fly-fishing and horseback rides through rocky passes. The only difference? The butler that awaits each evening to roast made-to-order s'mores around a roaring fire.

800/473-0601 or 406/244-5200; pawsup.com; doubles from $$$$$, including all meals.

The timber-clad
Grand Lodge at
Brush Creek Ranch.

LODGE & SPA AT BRUSH CREEK RANCH

NEARLY TWO CENTURIES AFTER MANIFEST DESTINY lured scores of American settlers to unknown frontiers, the West continues to hold the rest of the country in thrall. At the Lodge & Spa at Brush Creek Ranch, even the most dedicated urbanite can tap into the outback spirit. Sprawled over 13,000 acres in Wyoming's version of Big Sky Country, the working cattle ranch has plenty to offer in the way of active pursuits: rodeo lessons, ranger tours, and hunting parties for antelope, moose, and mountain lions. Rooms in log cabins come with heated bathroom floors, stone fireplaces, and 400-thread-count sheets, while healing treatments at the Trailhead Spa draw on Native American traditions (don't miss the smudging ritual, performed in an outdoor tepee). A home on the range never seemed so inviting.

66 Brush Creek Ranch Rd.; 307/327-5284; brushcreekranch.com; doubles from $$$$$, all-inclusive.

united states + canada

39

The Fireside Lounge at Four Seasons Resort Vail.

VAIL, COLORADO

FOUR SEASONS RESORT

PULLING OFF A NEW RESORT within the compact alpine village of Vail is no easy feat. While the footprint of this Four Seasons is relatively modest, the hotel itself is anything but. The eight-story, lodge-inspired structure overlooks an unlikely centerpiece: a 75-foot-long, heated outdoor saltwater pool. (Not to worry—just-warmed robes proffered by pool attendants make getting out of the water as pleasurable as getting in.) The lobby summons up a restrained mountain-chic aesthetic— think studded leather chairs, not antlers—as does the hickory-and-limestone spa. Still, what sets the Four Seasons apart is the high-altitude extras: walk-in closets for stashing bulky ski gear; fireplaces to temper those Rocky Mountain nights; and ski and boot fittings at check-in. Pick up your equipment from the ski concierge when you're ready to hit the slopes—and don't forget your free hand warmers.

1 Vail Rd.; 800/332-3442 or 970/477-8600; fourseasons.com; doubles from $$$.

PARK CITY, UTAH

MONTAGE DEER VALLEY

A whirlpool in Montage
Deer Valley's spa overlooks
the Uinta Mountains.

WITH SLOPES GROOMED TO A CORDUROY PERFECTION and oysters on the half
shell served in the trailside restaurant, the wintertime enclave of Deer
Valley makes no bones about spoiling its skiers. But leave it to the 220-room
Montage—mere steps from three high-speed chair lifts—to up the ante with
the largest spa in the state and iPad-equipped valets that do all the work for
you. (It's no wonder that the property was chosen to host the 2011 Sundance
Film Festival's opening-night gala.) But the revelry isn't reserved for the stars.
Four bars serving craft beers and a popular happy hour make it the valley's
go-to après-ski destination. And families aren't left out of the fun, thanks
to an arcade that's stocked with both Nintendo Wii and vintage video games
and features a four-lane bowling alley. Like every self-respecting ski resort,
the Montage has a mascot: Monty, a friendly Bernese mountain dog, who
makes regular appearances alongside complimentary cups of hot chocolate.

9100 Marsac Ave.; 866/551-8244 or 435/604-1300; montagedeervalley.com; doubles from $$$$.

41

ALLISON INN & SPA

THE WILLAMETTE VALLEY REVELS in its anti-Napa status. Forty-five minutes southwest of Portland, it has no big-name vineyards or rambling tour buses; its grape farmers and self-taught enologists aren't the sort to court publicity. But the wine-savvy crowd that's flocking to the LEED-certified Allison Inn—the valley's first hotel in which the phrase "thread count" comes into play—might just change all that. You'll find tangerine bath salts in the guest rooms, boutique teas in the lobby, and kinesis machines in the fitness center. The service is equally remarkable. Most impressive of all is the hotel's restaurant, Jory, headed by chef Sunny Jin, whose background includes stints at Spain's El Bulli and, yes, Napa Valley's French Laundry. It's a telling sign that this under-the-radar destination is officially ripe for discovery.

2525 Allison Lane; 877/294-2525 or 503/554-2525; theallison.com; doubles from $$.

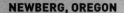

The Allison Inn & Spa, backed by the Willamette Valley's rolling vineyards.

LOS ANGELES

MR. C BEVERLY HILLS

A BELLINI WITH YOUR ROOM KEY? That's a given at Mr. C Beverly Hills. After all, the C stands for Cipriani, the family behind some of the world's most iconic restaurants and cocktail lounges. Brothers Ignazio and Maggio's first hotel, in the former Loews Tower, remains true to their Italian roots but capitalizes on Old Hollywood glamour: vintage black-and-white photos above burgundy chesterfield sofas; quilted leather headboards against neutral-toned walls. A lobby clad in travertine and rosewood leads not to a check-in desk (which is hidden from view) but to a Jazz Age–inspired bar. Private balconies in each suite overlook the teak pool deck, with its coral-and-white cabanas. One thing is certain: In a city where dramatic entrances are de rigueur, Mr. C has just made his.

1224 Beverwil Dr., Beverly Hills; 877/334-5623 or 301/277-2800; cipriani.com; doubles from $$.

Reclining, cabana-style, on the teak pool deck at Mr. C Beverly Hills.

A porter at work in the Redbury's lobby. Above: A street view of the hotel at night.

THE REDBURY

LOS ANGELES

THE REDBURY

NOTHING LASTS in the notoriously transient world of Tinseltown—but at the Redbury, you'll want your 15 minutes to go on as long as possible. Located at the nightlife nexus of Hollywood and Vine, developer Sam Nazarian's new hotel has all the buzz of his club-centric SBE brand. A 40-foot-high curtain of red velvet leads to hallways flanked by photos of Jimi Hendrix and Marilyn Monroe. Interiors are peppered with vintage turntables and flea-market finds, courtesy of the hotel's creative director, celebrity photographer Matthew Rolston, who imbued the apartment-style units with his rock-and-roll sensibility. Book bespoke guest services such as a Gibson guitar lesson or a stylist-guided shopping spree. Or join regulars like Jamie Foxx and Kanye West at the cocktail lounge known as the Library, and pretend you're one of the A-list.

1717 Vine St., Hollywood; 877/962-1717; theredbury.com; doubles from $$.

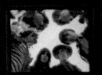

The breakfast
nook in a
Signature Flat at
the Redbury.

Seared ahi tuna with edamame-cilantro risotto at Koa Kea Boutique Hotel's Red Salt. Left: The restaurant's lounge.

KOA KEA BOUTIQUE HOTEL

THE GOLDEN CRESCENT OF POIPU, on Kauai's sunbaked southern coast, is a top contender for America's nicest beach—and judging from the number of mega-hotels and condos along the shore, more than a few people agree with that sentiment. Koa Kea Boutique Hotel offers a much more intimate way to experience this coveted stretch of sand. The resort forgoes the kid-friendly bells and whistles of bigger properties for simpler, more grown-up pleasures in its 121 rooms. Private lanais look out over the ocean; bathrooms come with L'Occitane products and multiple showerheads. Days roll by as you indulge in a rejuvenating ginger-and-jasmine flower body wrap and a lomilomi massage by the water; watch colorful marine life swim past you at one of the state's best snorkeling coves, a short walk away; or simply enjoy a pint of Maui Brewing Company's Big Swell IPA poolside at the hotel's thatched-roof tiki bar. The background couldn't be nicer.

2251 Poipu Rd.; 888/898-8958 or 808/828-8888; koakea.com; doubles from $$.

One of Koa Kea's
Ocean Front suites.

Makaala, the thatched-
roof lobby at the
Disney Aulani resort.

OAHU, HAWAII

DISNEY AULANI

LEAVE IT TO A PLACE with "imagineers" on the payroll to dream up a hotel like the Aulani, a sprawling, thatched-roof playground on Oahu's breezy coast. Unlike its princess-primping brethren, the Aulani supplants Disney's trademark whimsy with authenticity, giving visitors a native take on Hawaiian culture and tradition. That means tiki torches are out; local artwork, lamps made from gourds, and wood headboards inspired by outrigger canoes are in. As at any Disney lodging, families figure heavily into the target demographic, as evidenced by the hotel's expansive pool area, which includes a 900-foot-long lazy river, two winding waterslides, and a saltwater snorkeling lagoon stocked with hundreds of angelfish, tangs, and butterfly fish, plus plenty of coral. Adults might head to Laniwai spa's Puli Bar to create a custom wrap before retreating to the mineral baths and pools that make up the outdoor hydrotherapy garden.

92-1185 Aliinui Dr.; 866/443-4763 or 808/674-6200; resorts.disney.go.com; doubles from $$.

The resort's catamaran resting on the beach. Above: A young guest outside Aunty's Beach House activities club.

PORTUGAL COVE–ST. PHILIP'S, NEWFOUNDLAND

BEACH HOUSE

RUGGED AND PICTURESQUE, Canada's easternmost island typically calls to mind windswept landscapes and cozy fisherman's sweaters. Beach House, however, provides both sophistication and surprise. On a cliff above Conception Bay, the contemporary Cape-style structure has seven chocolate-hued suites with ocean-facing windows and private patios ideally situated for spotting minke and humpback whales. But the real draw is Atlantica, a restaurant that serves seasonal specialties such as roasted butternut squash bisque and bison carpaccio. Chef Steve Vardy has cooked for the likes of the Rolling Stones and Robert Plant—proof that even low-key Newfoundland possesses its own quiet sort of star power.

38 Beachy Cove Rd.; 800/895-3654 or 709/895-1250; atthebeachhouse.ca; doubles from $.

SOOKE HARBOUR HOUSE

BUCOLIC VANCOUVER ISLAND tends to keep a modest profile, even by Canadian standards. But the locavore food scene, with its vineyards, farms, and artisanal producers, is finally getting the attention it deserves. Much of that is thanks to Sooke Harbour House, a 28-room white-clapboard inn along the southern coast. At the on-site restaurant, the chef works wonders with a menu based almost exclusively on island ingredients: that means no olive oil and no produce that can't be grown in the garden. What *can* be grown here is remarkable, ranging from Asian pears and four varieties of kiwi to dozens of distinctly flavored geraniums, which taste of apple or dill or lime. Seafood is often the focus, whether it's a Dungeness crab soup or sweet Weathervane scallops gathered from the waters below the hotel. Further evidence of the inn's quirky foodie cred: charismatic owner Sinclair Philip curates a 10,000-bottle wine cellar and maintains a mushroom blog to boot.

1528 Whiffen Spit Rd.; 800/889-9688 or 250/642-3421; sookeharbourhouse.com; doubles from $$.

The garden-shaded entrance to Sooke Harbour House.

Walking up to Ian
Fleming's villa
at GoldenEye Hotel &
Resort, in Jamaica.

JAMAICADOMINICANREPUBLICPUERTORICOANGUILLAST
GRENADINESBARBADOSJAMAICADOMINICANREPUBLICPUE

CARIBBEAN

GoldenEye Hotel &
Resort's stone
patio overlooking
Low Cay Beach.

JAMAICA

GOLDENEYE HOTEL & RESORT

JET-SETTERS AND BOHEMIANS have flocked to GoldenEye since the mid 20th century, when it was Ian Fleming's cliff-top retreat. (The author wrote 14 of his James Bond novels here.) After a two-year overhaul courtesy of its current owner, Island Records founder Chris Blackwell, the 22-room property has morphed from private estate to full-fledged hotel. But thanks to Blackwell's highly personal touch, the concept remains the same: a tropical playground for well-traveled expats. Set amid coconut and mango trees, the shingled waterfront cottages—three are named for Bond vixens such as Vesper and Domino—have kitchen appliances by Renzo Piano and design flourishes from the mogul's stylish friends, including Barbara Hulanicki of Biba and Pink Sands fame. Fleming's original three-bedroom villa has also been spruced up and still spotlights the writer's own desk, carved out of Jamaican red bulletwood. At the resort's Bizot Bar, perched over Low Cay Beach, you can toast your surroundings with a martini—the bartender knows just how you'll take it.

Oracabessa Bay, St. Mary; 800/688-7678 or 876/622-9007; goldeneye.com; doubles from $$$$.

The restaurant's grilled lobster with jerk butter. Above: Looking out from a Lagoon suite.

Breezy *palapas* on Playa Las Terrenas, at Balcones del Atlántico.

DOMINICAN REPUBLIC

BALCONES DEL ATLÁNTICO, A ROCKRESORT

LEGEND HAS IT THAT UPON SETTING FOOT on the Samaná Peninsula in 1492, Christopher Columbus proclaimed it "the most beautiful land in the world." While the accuracy of that quote may be questionable, the allure of this spot on the Dominican Republic's northeastern coast is anything but. The area has rapidly become an ecotourism darling, thanks to a wealth of beaches, waterfalls, and tropical rain forest. At the center of it all is Balcones del Atlántico, on Playa Las Terrenas, where each of the 86 suites is a residence unto itself, measuring from 1,900 to more than 4,000 square feet of space. Filled with hand-carved teak furniture and beachy accents (ship's wheels; Balinese-stone sinks) and featuring fully stocked, ultramodern kitchens, they're indicative of a new level of sophistication on the peninsula. The real showstopper, however, is the sheer spectacle of wildlife: from January to March, up to 5,000 humpback whales convene just offshore, a sight best seen from the hotel's oceanfront restaurant.

Las Terrenas; 866/617-7625 or 809/240-5011; rockresorts.com; doubles from $$.

The balcony off
the Governor's Suite
at St. Regis
Bahia Beach Resort.

An outdoor lounge near the beach. Right: The library in the lobby.

PUERTO RICO

ST. REGIS BAHIA BEACH RESORT

WITH MORE THAN 100 BILLION GALLONS of precipitation each year, Puerto Rico's El Yunque rain forest seems an unlikely neighbor for a sunny seaside retreat. But nestled between the lush tropical canopy and the Atlantic Ocean lies the St. Regis Bahia Beach Resort. Preservation is a top priority: the 483-acre former coconut plantation serves as a private bird sanctuary recognized by Audubon International, and naturalists on staff guide expeditions along its serpentine nature trails. Still, this isn't exactly the heart of the jungle. There's an 18-hole golf course, a 10,000-square-foot Remède Spa, a kids' club that puts the focus on outdoor adventure, and an Afro-Caribbean restaurant with a menu by Jean-Georges Vongerichten. And Old San Juan, with its boutiques and bustling nightspots, is just a 40-minute drive away.

Km 4.2, Rte. 187, Rio Grande; 877/787-3447 or 787/809-8000; stregis.com; doubles from $$$$.

An aerial view of
the pool and gardens
at Anacaona
Boutique Hotel.

ANGUILLA

ANACAONA
BOUTIQUE
HOTEL

ON AN ISLAND OF $1,000-A-NIGHT RATES, the modestly priced Anacaona Boutique Hotel manages to feel like a splurge. The genius lies in the details, from the Frette linens to the free Wi-Fi in the 27 vibrant rooms. Two pools on the grounds seem almost superfluous given the resort's pristine mile-long shoreline. Another reason to take to the sand: waiters deliver fruity rum punch or an ice-cold Ting at a wave of your hand. Despite these courtesies, owners Robin and Sue Ricketts, whose backgrounds include stints at Cap Juluca and Malliouhana, chose to forgo a glitzy resort experience for a simpler, more authentic emphasis on island traditions. Local historians and artists are invited to give talks; on Thursday nights, a West Indian folkloric troupe performs dances and songs passed down through generations. Judging from its popularity, Anacaona has struck a chord.

Meads Bay; 877/647-4736 or 264/497-6827; anacaonahotel.com; doubles from $.

caribbean

61

Lounging poolside
at La Banane.

LA BANANE

WITH ITS SPLASHY VILLAS and star-studded following, St. Bart's is a natural setting for this stylishly revamped hotel. Once owned by the late cabaret impresario Jean-Marie Rivière, La Banane was known for nightly performances featuring showgirls and drag queens. Now it has reemerged as a Midcentury Modern–inspired refuge with camera-ready vignettes at every turn. Two pools give way to nine white bungalows with pastel walls, geometric floor tiles, and teak and rosewood furniture designed by Swiss-born architect Pierre Jeanneret for his cousin Le Corbusier. Alfresco showers and private patios overlook floral gardens buzzing with hummingbirds. The ace in the hole is the lively Chandi' Bar, where crowds gather for a weekly flamenco dance party that channels Monsieur Rivière at his flamboyant best.

Baie de Lorient; 590-590/520-300; labanane.com; doubles from $$$.

The Juliette Deluxe Bungalow. Above: Plush seating in the outdoor lounge.

caribbean

63

ANTIGUA

FOR A PLACE WITH AS MANY PICTURESQUE beaches as there are days in the year, Antigua has remained a little-known gem. Now you can take advantage of its under-the-radar status at hotels that vary between iconically grand and unassumingly sporty.

1 JUMBY BAY, A ROSEWOOD RESORT

After a $28 million overhaul, all-inclusive Jumby Bay is luring the rich and famous once more. On a private island just off the mainland, the resort now has a Euro-Caribbean restaurant serving freshly caught fish and local produce, an ocean-facing infinity pool, and an alfresco spa where treatments include indigenous elements such as coconut milk, bamboo, pink coral, and sugarcane.

ROOM TO BOOK Stay in a Beachside Courtyard suite, which has vaulted ceilings, sitting areas in the bathroom, and an outdoor soaking tub and mosaic-tile shower set in a secluded garden. **DON'T MISS** Afternoon buffets at the Verandah Kitchen feature several varieties of finger sandwiches and iced tea, all best enjoyed after a rousing game of croquet on the lawn of the 1830's Estate House.

Long Island; 888/767-3966 or 268/462-6000; rosewoodhotels.com; doubles from $$$$$.

A suite on the private-island resort of Jumby Bay.

2 SUGAR RIDGE

High in the hills above picturesque Jolly Harbour, Sugar Ridge resort makes up for its lack of shoreline with spectacular Caribbean views (a shuttle takes guests to nearby beaches three times a day). Muslin-draped beds, honey-colored marble bathrooms, and garden terraces are par for the course. The hotel is also home to the Caribbean's first Aveda Concept Spa. **ROOM TO BOOK** Lower-floor rooms have king-size four-poster beds, open-air dining decks, and personal plunge pools. **DON'T MISS** The breezy hilltop restaurant Carmichael's has become a gathering place for locals and expats. They go for the fresh seafood and knockout desserts, such as bread-and-butter pudding with Antiguan rum sauce and coconut rice with mango purée.

Tottenham Park, St. Mary; 866/591-4881; sugarridgeantigua.com; doubles from $$.

3 NONSUCH BAY

Pro skippers favor the calm waters off Nonsuch Bay, on one of the island's eastern bluffs. In the evening, the sailing set stays at this remote resort, a collection of Georgian-inspired villas and wood-shingled apartments set among 40 acres of gardens. French windows throughout let in plenty of light; high ceilings and wraparound verandas add to the hotel's airy ambience. **ROOM TO BOOK** The 1,400-square-foot beach cottages sit just behind Nonsuch's private strip of palm-fringed sand. Designer kitchens come with modern conveniences such as dishwashers and washer-dryers. **DON'T MISS** Activities range from exclusive sailing classes and kite-surfing school to guided snorkeling trips along neighboring Green Island's coral reef.

Hughes Point, St. Philip; 888/844-2480 or 268/562-8000; nonsuchbayresort.com; doubles from $$.

The pool area at whitewashed Sugar Ridge.

The Asian-inspired Bay restaurant overlooking Nonsuch Bay's blue waters.

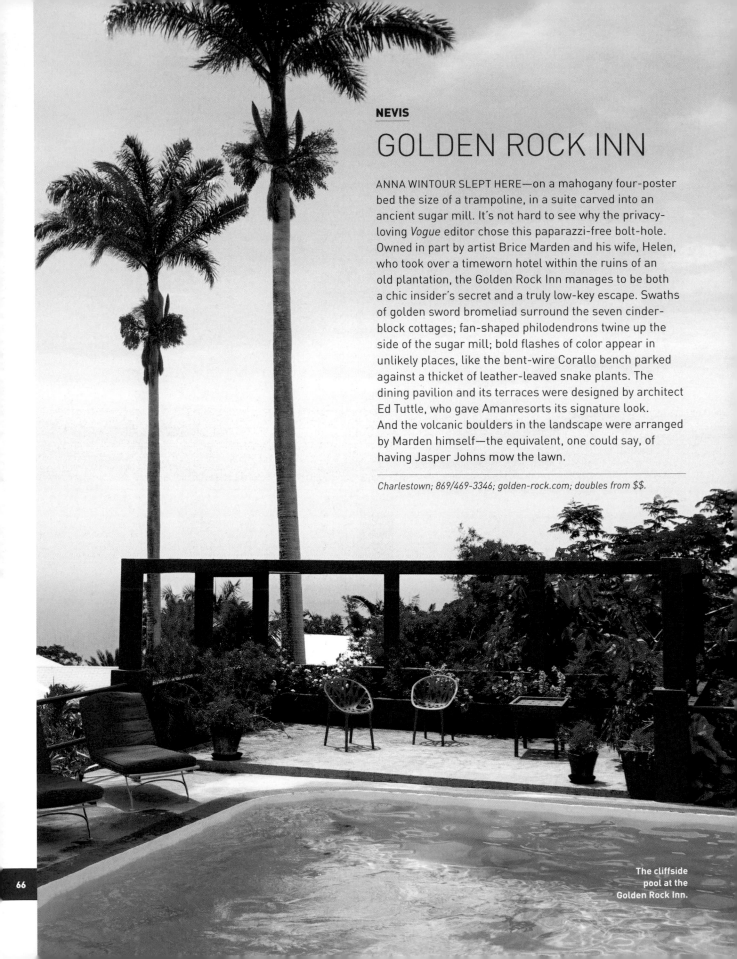

NEVIS

GOLDEN ROCK INN

ANNA WINTOUR SLEPT HERE—on a mahogany four-poster bed the size of a trampoline, in a suite carved into an ancient sugar mill. It's not hard to see why the privacy-loving *Vogue* editor chose this paparazzi-free bolt-hole. Owned in part by artist Brice Marden and his wife, Helen, who took over a timeworn hotel within the ruins of an old plantation, the Golden Rock Inn manages to be both a chic insider's secret and a truly low-key escape. Swaths of golden sword bromeliad surround the seven cinder-block cottages; fan-shaped philodendrons twine up the side of the sugar mill; bold flashes of color appear in unlikely places, like the bent-wire Corallo bench parked against a thicket of leather-leaved snake plants. The dining pavilion and its terraces were designed by architect Ed Tuttle, who gave Amanresorts its signature look. And the volcanic boulders in the landscape were arranged by Marden himself—the equivalent, one could say, of having Jasper Johns mow the lawn.

Charlestown; 869/469-3346; golden-rock.com; doubles from $$.

The cliffside pool at the Golden Rock Inn.

The ocean-facing Coralita villa at Turtle Beach Bungalows.

ST. KITTS

TURTLE BEACH BUNGALOWS

ALTHOUGH TURTLE BEACH BUNGALOWS is part of Christophe Harbour—ultimately destined to become a 2,500-acre development with a beach club, a marina, and an 18-hole, Tom Fazio–designed golf course—it feels like a genuine hideaway. Four cottages made of reclaimed pine and bamboo stretch along the sand dunes on a quiet peninsula surrounded by turquoise waters. Wooden shutters fold back to expose floor-to-ceiling glass doors and patios with direct ocean access; cabanas and copper-clad outdoor showers beckon after a swim in the sea. Evenings are best spent at Beach House, the hotel's restaurant, where the seafood comes fresh from the Basseterre market. After dinner take a plunge in your bungalow's private pool, gazing at the glimmering lights of Nevis on the horizon.

Christophe Harbour; 800/881-7180 or 869/466-4557; turtlebeachbungalows.com; doubles from $$$$.

caribbean

67

A view of the Pitons from the infinity pool at Hotel Chocolat's Club Boucan lounge.

ST. LUCIA

HOTEL CHOCOLAT

THE SOUTH SEAS–LIKE LANDSCAPE of St. Lucia's Soufrière district is made even more dramatic by the Pitons, those two conical mountains that rise up where the jungle meets the ocean. In their shadow lies Hotel Chocolat, 14 villas on a cacao-growing plantation aiming to turn cocoa farming into a sustainable industry. Interiors are awash in chocolate hues—from the espresso-colored floorboards to the milky stucco walls—and the scent of guava, banana, and papaya trees perfumes the air. By day, embark on a fruit-tasting safari, indulge in a cocoa oil massage, or visit the on-site chocolate factory. At night, the warble of tree frogs provides the sound track to a meal at the hotel's Boucan Restaurant. The fitting end to your feast: mousse made with the estate's latest chocolate cuvée.

Rabot Estate, Soufrière; 800/757-7132; thehotelchocolat.com; doubles from $$.

ST. VINCENT AND THE GRENADINES

PETIT ST. VINCENT RESORT

THIS PRIVATE-ISLAND RESORT has always been as exclusive as it gets. You might never see another guest during your stay on the palm-studded islet in the Grenadines archipelago, where a hammock-strewn beach encircles a lushly forested interior. But after a multimillion-dollar overhaul, the 115-acre Petit St. Vincent takes escapism to a whole new level. The 22 pitched-roof cottages now have wooden sundecks and outdoor showers, but true to PSV tradition, there are still no phones or TV's. That's not to say that diversions are in short supply. The new owners added a driftwood-timber spa pavilion and a 49-foot sailing sloop for custom charters. And service is as highly attuned as ever: a yellow flag hoisted outside your cottage summons the staff when you want them; a red one keeps them at bay when you don't.

Petit St. Vincent; 800/654-9326; psvresort.com; doubles from $$$$$.

One of the stone cottages at Petit St. Vincent Resort.

Fairmont Royal
Pavilion's pool
and gardens.

BARBADOS

FAIRMONT ROYAL PAVILION

WHEN THE FAIRMONT ROYAL PAVILION MADE ITS DEBUT in the 1940's, it was the finest resort on Barbados's western coast. Now the palatial pink grande dame is tops once again, after a renovation that fused colonial style with Caribbean cool. Cream-colored walls and rich walnut furnishings reflect the island's plantation-house heritage; the picturesque Palm Terrace Restaurant upholds the new Bajan reputation for eclectic cuisine in dishes such as apple-cinnamon pork tenderloin with Chinese eggplant *pico de gallo*. Afternoon tea is served in the best British tradition, featuring a succession of scones, cakes, and finger sandwiches that would please the queen herself.

Porters, St. James; 800/441-1414 or 246/422-5555; fairmont.com; doubles from $$$$.

caribbean

The Atlantic-facing
Playa Vik, in
José Ignacio, Uruguay.

MEXICO + CENTRAL + SOUTH AMERICA

OSAIRESSALTAPUNTADELESTEMALDONADO+ROCHACARMELO
EBUENOSAIRESSALTAPUNTADELESTEMALDONADO+ROCHA

Delivering
breakfast
at Rosewood
San Miguel
de Allende.

SAN MIGUEL DE ALLENDE, MEXICO

ROSEWOOD

HISTORY IS EVER-PRESENT on the cobblestoned streets of San Miguel de Allende, lending the city much of its celebrated charm. The same magic is at work inside Rosewood's colonial-inspired hacienda, the area's first international luxury resort. Pieces by local artisans are displayed at every turn: patios and colonnades are crafted of *cantera* stone, while curled wooden bedposts and ornate tin-framed mirrors grace the guest rooms—some of which look out onto the Gothic spires of La Parroquia church. Age-old culinary traditions live on at the 1826 Restaurant, where such dishes as suckling pig with sage and Mexican squash ravioli make a bold locavore statement. At the rooftop bar, hibiscus and tamarind margaritas pay homage to San Miguel's vibrantly colored façades. Prefer your spirits with a bit more bite? One of the hotel's 120-plus tequilas should fill the bill.

11 Nemesio Diez; 888/767-3966 or 52-41/5152-9700; rosewoodhotels.com; doubles from $$.

Overlooking La Parroquia, in Plaza Allende. Above: A Deluxe Colonial guest room.

Books on display in Condesa DF's Culture Room. Right: Condé, the resident chocolate lab.

CONDESA DF

THE DISTRITO FEDERAL'S CHAOTIC HAZE DISSIPATES in the leafy enclave of Condesa, whose tree-lined streets, cafés, and galleries feel practically Parisian. Fittingly, it was a Paris-based interior designer, India Mahdavi, who restyled a 1928 Neoclassical building into the 40-room Condesa DF, introducing a bohemian aesthetic that's wholly in keeping with the neighborhood. The new look juxtaposes indigenous materials (Oaxacan blankets; alpaca-wool carpets) with sculptural space-age tables, Midcentury-inspired furnishings, and striking turquoise walls. The hotel heats up at night, when the rooftop sushi bar and basement dance club become the hottest spots in town. Word of advice: after a late night, order the signature *chilaquiles*—a traditional Mexican hangover remedy—for a restorative room-service breakfast.

102 Avda. Veracruz; 866/978-7020 or 52-55/5241-2600; condesadf.com; doubles from $.

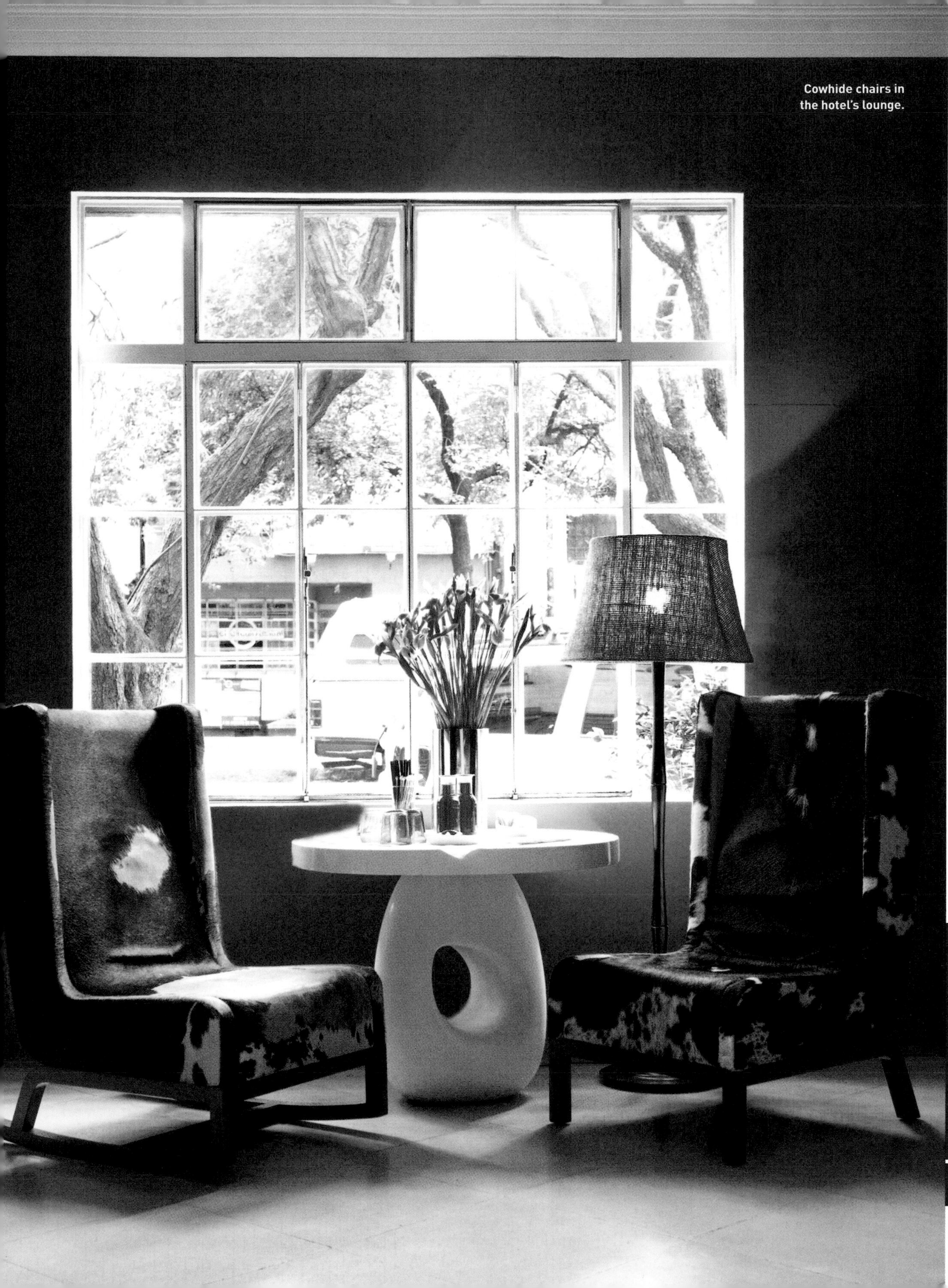

Cowhide chairs in the hotel's lounge.

Hotel Encanto's
pool and
Lounge Bar.

ACAPULCO, MEXICO

HOTEL ENCANTO

NINE YEARS—that's how long it took architect Miguel Ángel Aragonés to complete his all-white Hotel Encanto, with a cool exterior that is the perfect contrast to Acapulco's sultry heat. Emerging from a hilltop near Puerto Marqués, the 44-room property is a geometric ode to the sea, a symphony of flat planes and rounded portholes angled and arranged to echo the fluidity of water. During the day, private terraces and glass walls offer both fleeting glimpses of and lingering looks at the Pacific. At night, the hotel is bathed in eye-catching hues, in keeping with the architect's predilection for bold lighting. The bar and pool deck, on the other hand, are illuminated simply by candles, mirroring the starry panorama overhead.

51 Jacques Cousteau; 52-744/446-7101; hotelencanto. com.mx; doubles from $$.

The hotel's view of Puerto Marqués Bay. Above: An Encanto suite.

HOTEL PARACAS

AGAINST THE RUGGED LANDSCAPE of the Paracas Peninsula, where rainfall is scarce and the wildlife spectacular, the whitewashed Hotel Paracas evokes a coastal desert version of *Miami Vice*. And no wonder: it was designed by the Miami-based firm Arquitectonica, which is headed by Peruvian-born architect Bernardo Fort-Brescia. Rooms with private bamboo terraces face the sea; at a cabana-surrounded heated pool by water's edge, expertly mixed pisco sours are always just a bartender away. As the current weekend spot for Lima's elite and a jumping-off point to the region, the property is unmatched. You can spy flamingos and Humboldt penguins at the Paracas Nature Reserve, explore the Incan ruins at Tambo Colorado, or marvel at sea lions on a day trip to the Islas Ballestas, often compared to Ecuador's Galápagos.

173 Avda. Paracas, Ica; 800/325-3589 or 51-56/581-333; luxurycollection.com; doubles from $$.

The teak pool deck and lounge at Hotel Paracas.

TAMBO DEL INKA

CRAMPED TOURIST TRAINS OR MULTIDAY TREKS were once the only ways to reach Machu Picchu. Tambo del Inka offers a much more refined alternative. The Sacred Valley's most celebrated luxury hotel, an hour from Cuzco, puts ease at the forefront in every respect—from a private train station that gives you direct service to the ruins to a concierge who organizes artisan village tours and rafting trips down the Ollantaytambo river. A massive double-sided fireplace inspired by ancient stone walls commands the lobby; in the restaurant, traditional elements like *quipus* (knots of fabric used by the Incas as accounting aids) serve both as design motifs and the backdrop for native dishes that showcase produce from area farmers. At the spa, treatments are regal enough for an Incan princess, with ingredients like coca, cacao, and even 24-karat gold.

Avda. Ferrocarril; 800/325-3589 or 51-84/581-777; luxurycollection.com; doubles from $$.

An aerial view
of Tambo del
Inka and the
Vilcanota River.

Inside Le Rêve Hotel Boutique's courtyard. Right: A rich leather headboard in one of the guest rooms.

SANTIAGO, CHILE

LE RÊVE HOTEL BOUTIQUE

A REFRESHING CHANGE FROM BOOMTOWN Santiago's soaring skyscraper hotels, the 31-room Le Rêve possesses a charmingly scaled-back sensibility. Behind the Francophile exterior of shutter-lined windows and wrought-iron railings, Chilean-born designer Sergio Echeverría envisioned an exquisitely decorated jewel box with a residential feel. Furnishings, which include claw-foot velvet settees, Tiffany lamps, and gold-framed antique maps, create a cocooning effect. (Book room No. 210 for its garden view and floor-to-ceiling French doors.) Tea and croissants can be taken in the pebbled courtyard in the shade of a hundred-year-old avocado tree. And what could be more inviting than a fully stocked, help-yourself pantry to satisfy late-night hunger pangs? It's enough to make you want to be a permanent guest.

23 Orrego Luco; 56-2/757-6000; lerevehotel.cl; doubles from $$.

The hotel's French-inspired entrance.

Decks overlooking the
Pacific Ocean at
Crusoe Island Lodge.

CRUSOE ISLAND LODGE

EIGHTEENTH-CENTURY SAILOR ALEXANDER SELKIRK spent four years stranded on this speck of land, inspiring the novel *Robinson Crusoe*. Civilization has since come to the once-uninhabited isle, but the spirit of adventure endures at Crusoe Island Lodge—reached only after a two-hour flight on a seven-seat plane from Santiago followed by a speedboat ride to the town of San Juan Bautista, then a short drive to Bahía Pangal cove. Positioned dramatically along the rocky shore, the 15 rooms are made of recycled materials and wood from the nearby forest, with raw-canvas hammocks on terraces overlooking the surf. The castaway life this is not: you can book a pearl-powder facial at the spa or taste a flight of Chilean wines at the restaurant. Still, there are plenty of opportunities to tap into more primitive pleasures, including deep-sea fishing, shipwreck diving, or trekking through the rain forest to the lookout where Selkirk scanned the horizon for—and eventually found—rescue.

Bahía Pangal; 56-23/460-103; crusoeislandlodge.com; doubles from $$$, all-inclusive.

A vintage Rönisch piano in the entrance hall at Magnolia Hotel Boutique.

BUENOS AIRES

MAGNOLIA HOTEL BOUTIQUE

TUCKED AMONG THE EARLY-20TH-CENTURY town houses in the fashionable Palermo neighborhood, this restored hotel channels the romanticism of Argentina's golden era. Hardwood floors, antique wardrobes, and handcrafted tables make for a discreetly luxe vibe in the eight bedrooms; historic elements blend with indigenous touches, such as the original stained-glass ceiling that sets off the lobby's cheeky cowhide ottomans. House-made pastries, jams, and yogurts, eggs cooked to order, and the ubiquitous *dulce de leche* are served each morning in the tiled courtyard, adding to the atmosphere of domestic comfort. In bustling Buenos Aires, the Magnolia is a true hidden gem.

1746 Julián Álvarez; 54-11/4867-4900; magnoliahotel. com.ar; doubles from $.

Local jams offered in a room-service breakfast spread. Above: A daybed on the roof terrace.

FIERRO HOTEL PALERMO

IN A NEIGHBORHOOD THAT HAS BECOME GROUND ZERO for the city's restaurant renaissance, the Fierro Hotel Palermo has an ace up its sleeve in native-born chef Hernán Gipponi. The Guggenheim Bilbao alum dishes out haute cuisine that is a refreshing change of pace from the meat-heavy staples around town and is highlighted by a nine-course tasting menu (halibut with quinoa and asparagus; Spanish rice with squid and sweet onions) paired with wines from the restaurant's staggering cellar. After your meal, the ultramodern hotel serves as a low-key urban crash pad with 27 rooms outfitted in angular furnishings and abstract artwork, and stocked with personal iPads—all the better for making your next reservation.

5862 Soler; 54-11/3220-6800; fierrohotel.com; doubles from $.

Seating in Fierro Hotel Palermo's lobby.

A shaded open-air lounge at House of Jasmines Estancia de Charme.

SALTA, ARGENTINA

HOUSE OF JASMINES ESTANCIA DE CHARME

IN THE UNTAMED LAND OF GAUCHO LEGENDS, on a 300-acre ranch shadowed by the Andes Mountains, the delicate scent of jasmine may be incongruous but is not at all unwelcome. Once the private estancia of actor Robert Duvall, the ivy-covered House of Jasmines was transformed into a whitewashed inn that evokes a South American version of shabby-chic by a French family (who also created the refined Estancia El Colibrí). The 14 rooms feature hand-stitched linens, local handwoven rugs, and tufted headboards; the sweet-smelling shrubs that give the property its name are joined by a fruit orchard and vegetable gardens, which provide many of the ingredients for the inn's restaurant. Snag one of the sofas around the huge open hearth and savor a glass of Torrontés, a crisp regional white that pairs surprisingly well with the kitchen's hearty Andean fare.

Km 11, Ruta Nacional No. 51, La Merced Chica; 54-387/497-2002; houseofjasmines.com; doubles from $.

The organic pool deck at Fasano Las Piedras. Below: Coffee and sweets at the hotel's restaurant.

PUNTA DEL ESTE, URUGUAY

FASANO LAS PIEDRAS

THIS SPALIKE RETREAT, the first property outside Brazil from the cult-favorite Fasano Hotel brand, offers a meditative respite from Punta del Este's glitzy beach scene. Set on 1,000 acres of grassland facing a bird-filled estuary and pine forest, the hotel's stone-and-granite bungalows appear to be carved directly into the landscape. Earthy interiors—which have serious design cred, courtesy of Brazilian architect Isay Weinfeld—are brimming with organic textures: wood-paneled walls, sheepskin rugs, leather headboards. Even the pool conforms to the terrain, weaving its way among age-old rock formations that add to the tranquil mood. Yearning for champagne bottle service or the click of stilettos against pavement? Punta is just a short ride away.

La Barra; 598/4267-0000; fasano.com.br; doubles from $$$.

MALDONADO + ROCHA, URUGUAY

WITH HIGH-RISE PUNTA DEL ESTE ACTING AS A SOUTHERN Hemisphere clone of Miami Beach, a quieter scene is emerging elsewhere in the fisherman's villages of the Maldonado and Rocha districts. From upscale José Ignacio to the untouched landscapes of Garzón and La Pedrera, 80 miles away, here's the inside scoop on where to stay next.

1 PLAYA VIK

Designed by Uruguayan architect Carlos Ott, José Ignacio's Modernist Playa Vik makes a bold visual statement that stands in stark contrast to its sister hotel, the rustic-chic Estancia Vik, five miles inland. Art is at the forefront throughout: an angular, titanium-clad building dubbed the Sculpture and its cantilevered pool deck face the calm waters of the Atlantic Ocean; sculptor Pablo Atchugarry's massive bronze doors greet you at the building's entrance. **ROOM TO BOOK** Sleeping in one of the Sculpture's four guest rooms is like staying in a private gallery. Opt for the Valentina Suite, where Marcelo Legrand's graphic black-and-white fresco graces the bathroom's walls. **DON'T MISS** Each evening, guests gather around the *brasero*, an open fire pit, for unparalleled views of the stars.

Calle de los Cisnes y los Horneros, José Ignacio; 598/9460-5212; playavik.com; doubles from $$$$.

Sunset near the Sculpture, at Playa Vik.

❷ EL GARZÓN

From famed Argentine chef Francis Mallmann comes El Garzón, an intimate restaurant-with-rooms that resembles a friend's antiques-filled house. In a brick single-level hacienda on the corner of Pueblo Garzón's tiny plaza, five bedrooms face a lush garden and alfresco bar. In keeping with the area's equine history, horseback riding is included in your stay. **ROOM TO BOOK** The suites are all the same at El Garzón, with king-size beds, frosted-glass private bathrooms, and cozy wood-burning *chimeneas*. **DON'T MISS** The 50-seat restaurant feels less like a temple of refined cuisine than the study of a gentleman explorer. Local beef and poultry and vegetables from the garden are cooked *al infiernillo* (an Andean technique using two wood fires) and go to the table on sizzling iron griddles.

Garzón; 598/410-2811; restaurantegarzon.com; doubles from $$$, including meals.

❸ BRISAS DE LA PEDRERA

Brisas de La Pedrera is the oldest place to stay in the sleepy coastal village of La Pedrera, known for its superb sportfishing. Reborn after an extensive renovation, the 14-room hotel has all the hallmarks of a modern boutique: Egyptian-cotton sheets, Midcentury-inspired furniture, and reliable Wi-Fi service. **ROOM TO BOOK** Second-floor Zen Master suites feature floor-to-ceiling windows and walk-out terraces overlooking pristine Desplayado Beach and the windswept dunes of Cabo Polonio. Semiprivate seating areas bordered by shady eucalyptus trees stand out in the first-floor Jardin suites. **DON'T MISS** You can enjoy a massage or facial in the privacy of your own room. Active types might prefer horseback riding and hiking along the shore or hitting the waves freestyle.

La Pedrera; 598/4479-2265; brisasdelapedrera.com; doubles from $.

Window seating in El Garzón's restaurant.

A quiet patio at Brisas de La Pedrera.

Overlooking the Río de la Plata at Four Seasons Resort Carmelo.

CARMELO, URUGUAY

FOUR SEASONS RESORT

A PLEASANT SENSE of cognitive dissonance greets you upon arrival at the Four Seasons Resort Carmelo, a Southeast Asian–inspired hotel on a quiet swath of the eucalyptus-lined Río de la Plata. Intricately carved wooden doors and Far Eastern artifacts lend the high-ceilinged lobby a serene feel, while Pura, the batik-draped restaurant, features a Balinese spirit house surrounded by a mosaic-tiled pool. Most dishes, however, are resolutely Uruguayan: an indoor barbecue pit turns out mouthwatering asado, while traditional *empanaditas* and *tostadas de campo* using organic ingredients are given a gourmet spin. (A pastry chef is also on hand to teach guests how to make *alfajores*, the irresistible *dulce de leche*–filled pastries.) Polo lessons, fishing trips, and excursions to the UNESCO World Heritage site of Colonia can all be arranged—although lounging by the fire in the library, on a Siberian tiger–patterned rug, is a tempting alternative.

Km 262, Ruta 21; 800/332-3442 or 598/4542-9000; fourseasons.com; doubles from $$.

One of the hotel's spacious River-View bungalows.

BARRA DE SÃO MIGUEL, BRAZIL

KENOA

IT WAS A RISKY PROPOSITION for an engineer with zero hotel experience to quit his career and follow his dream of opening an eco-retreat along Brazil's northern coast. But one year later, Pedro Marques's gamble has paid off. At the 23-room Kenoa, located on a sleepy beach in Alagoa, the transition between indoors and out is virtually seamless, thanks to floor-to-ceiling windows that maximize ocean vistas, as well as natural wood-and-brick interiors supported by stately eucalyptus columns. Above all, environmental responsibility is key: sustainable solar heating, energy-efficient LED lights, and the use of salvaged building materials have kept the surrounding ecological preserve practically undisturbed. Sybaritic extras—the spa; the restaurant and wine bar; the waterfront infinity pools that echo the horizon—do little to undermine the endeavor. The result is a place where visitors are encouraged to breathe deeply while they tread softly.

58 Rua Escritor Jorge de Lima, Barramar; 55-82/3272-1285; kenoaresort.com; doubles from $$$.

Shrimp *moqueca* (stew), served at the hotel's Kaamo restaurant. Above: The bedroom in an Apoena suite.

mexico + central + south america

The Queen's Chair restaurant at Aman Sveti Stefan, overlooking Montenegro's Budva Bay.

EDINBURGHIRELANDLONDONLISBONALENTEJORIOJABAR
FLORENCESARDINIACAPRIPUGLIAAMSTERDAMHAMBURG

EUROPE

ONAMAJORCACAPFERRETPARISAUVERGNEMILANVENICE
INSTOCKHOLMMONTENEGROATHENSMESSENIAISTANBUL

The 1739 exterior of Hotel du Vin Edinburgh.

EDINBURGH
HOTEL DU VIN

IF THESE WALLS COULD TALK. What was once a city asylum is now giving refuge to a different sort of resident: locavores on a relative budget. Occupying a 1739 stone building in the heart of Old Town, the Hotel du Vin Edinburgh has a decidedly modern air beyond its medieval-looking entry. Think purple fleur-de-lis wall coverings, color-coordinated tartan throw pillows, and a lobby chandelier made of wineglasses. Details like rolltop copper soaking tubs and wooden beams add a touch of luxury to the 47 rooms. At the hotel's restaurant, chef Matt Powell serves such innovative Scottish dishes as smoked haddock cassoulet in an intimate dining room punctuated by original brick columns. Postprandial indulgences await in the leather-and-wood cigar room and whisky snug, a clubby space where the national drink monopolizes the conversation.

11 Bristo Place; 44-131/247-4900; hotelduvin.com; doubles from $$.

The Willi Opitz
Room, named
after the Austrian
winemaker.

The opulent
Westmeath
Bedroom
at Ballyfin.

Family portraits
along the wall of the
manor's cantilevered
main staircase.

COUNTY LAOIS, IRELAND

BALLYFIN

SET IN THE FOOTHILLS OF THE SLIEVE BLOOM MOUNTAINS, 60 miles southwest of Dublin, the Neoclassical mansion of Ballyfin was erected in 1826 to trumpet the wealth of the Premier Baronet of Ireland. When his family fell on hard times after World War I, so did the estate. Now the grande dame has all the refinement of a country manor once more: experts reconstructed the crumbling sandstone façade; plasterwork details were meticulously restored; and gilded antiques—mirrors by Thomas Chippendale; original portraits—again grace its colonnaded reception halls. The staff flurries about during afternoon tea, served in an 80-foot-long library with a fireplace at either end. For the royal treatment, though, stay in the fanciful Westmeath Bedroom, dominated by a carved French bed with a domed canopy of cream silk tethered to a golden frame.

Ballyfin; 353-57/875-5866; ballyfin.com; doubles from $$$$$, including meals.

LONDON

THE CROSSROADS OF EVERYTHING AND everywhere, London feels like the capital of the world right now. Just in time for the 2012 Olympics, the latest hotel openings reflect its wildly different personalities—monied extravagance, high-tech charm, Gothic splendor.

1 ST. PANCRAS RENAISSANCE HOTEL

Eurostar commuters have a dramatic new crash pad: St. Pancras Station, where the trains terminate. The architectural equivalent of a Brontë novel, the turreted station-hotel is made up of the original Victorian building, which houses 38 idiosyncratic rooms (Gothic windows; ornate plaster moldings) and a new wing with 207 sleek accommodations— all part of a historic renovation that cost more than $300 million. **ROOM TO BOOK** In the old building, Chambers suites have exclusive access to a private club. Opt for one with a view of the glass-and-steel Barlow train shed. **DON'T MISS** Try Carmelo Guastella's soothing 45-minute wet shave— a series of hot towels, creams, and straight razors—at chic men's barbershop Melogy.

Euston Rd.; 888/236-2427 or 44-20/7841-3540; marriott.com; doubles from $$.

Original detailing in one of St. Pancras Renaissance Hotel's Chambers suites.

2 W HOTEL LONDON, LEICESTER SQUARE

Hundreds of reflective disco balls hanging in the lobby greet you as you enter the trendy W London, behind an inscrutable white-glass exterior that changes colors throughout the day. There's always a party on the banquette-lined reception floor as well as in Jean-Georges Vongerichten's superb Spice Market. And the edgy staff is referred to as "the talent."

ROOM TO BOOK Studio-style Wonderful rooms feature an open-plan bedroom and bathroom, with the shower and commode hidden by mirrored double doors. **DON'T MISS** Things really heat up after midnight at the red-and-black VIP bar Wyld, which has hosted the likes of Kate Moss, Colin Firth, and Helena Bonham Carter. Ask the concierge to put your name on the list.

10 Wardour St.; 877/946-8357 or 44-20/7758-1000; whotels.com; doubles from $$.

3 CORINTHIA HOTEL, LONDON

The Corinthia Hotel is appropriately grand given its location in a former government building on tony Whitehall Place. About half a billion dollars were spent on details like elevator doors worthy of Ruhlmann, a massive Baccarat chandelier in the lobby, marble and limestone baths, and dressing rooms lined in French oak. **ROOM TO BOOK** Standout features in the Belle

Époque–inspired Explorers' Penthouse include double-height ceilings, parquet flooring, hand-finished rugs, two fireplaces, and a private roof terrace. **DON'T MISS** Sample cod tartare with capers or gray-snapper ceviche at the Massimo Restaurant & Oyster Bar, known as much for its variety of seafood as for the David Collins interiors.

Whitehall Place; 877/842-6269 or 44-20/7930-8181; corinthia.com; doubles from $$$.

The entrance to the W Hotel London, Leicester Square.

The Corinthia Hotel's restored Victorian façade.

▣ ECCLESTON SQUARE HOTEL

In Pimlico, where shabby B&B's still fill the backstreets around Victoria Station, the Eccleston Square Hotel has become a haven for the style set. Its Georgian face belies an ultramodern approach to the interiors: 3-D movies are screened on a 103-inch television in the media lounge; rooms are stocked with personal iPad 2's; bathroom mirrors are embedded with digital television screens; and "smart glass" walls go from clear to privacy-inducing cloudy at the touch of a button. **ROOM TO BOOK** Garden Queen rooms overlook a private green space, reserved for hotel guests and neighboring residents. **DON'T MISS** A Sunday American brunch with fresh-baked pastries, Tex-Mex omelettes, and blueberry pancakes is served in the Bistrot on the Square restaurant.

37 Eccleston Square; 44-20/3489-1000; ecclestonsquarehotel.com; doubles from $$.

Map labels:
REGENT'S PARK
1
LEICESTER SQUARE
WEST END
2
HYDE PARK
TRAFALGAR SQUARE
5
3
6
BUCKINGHAM PALACE
THAMES RIVER
4

A view of Eccleston Square Hotel from a private garden nearby.

5 45 PARK LANE

The Thierry Despont–designed 45 Park Lane, located across the street from its older sibling the Dorchester, recently opened as a more intimate and contemporary version of its glitzy predecessor. All of the 45 rooms have an updated Art Deco flavor, with tinted mirrors, cerused mahogany, and patterned carpeting that calls to mind the Duke of Windsor's argyles and plus fours.

ROOM TO BOOK Sleek Bang & Olufsen televisions aside, what sets two of the eighth-floor Executive King rooms apart are the expansive balconies overlooking Hyde Park.
DON'T MISS Wolfgang Puck has opened his first European restaurant here, importing his Beverly Hills standby, Cut. The steak house specializes in dry- and wet-aged beef in an elegant wood-paneled dining room.

45 Park Lane; 800/650-1842 or 44-20/7493-4545; dorchestercollection.com; doubles from $$$$.

6 FOUR SEASONS HOTEL LONDON AT PARK LANE

Luxury is to be expected in the Four Seasons Hotel London at Park Lane, reopened in the heart of Mayfair after a head-to-toe redo by Pierre-Yves Rochon. Rooms have the signature Four Seasons calm, but everywhere else the volume has been turned way up: tartans and zebra prints, a red-lacquer piano, and vibrant Arne Jacobsen furniture prove eye-catching in the lobby and lounge.

ROOM TO BOOK Top-floor Superior rooms have walnut-veneer walls, beige marble bathrooms, and far-reaching vistas of either Hyde Park or Westminster.
DON'T MISS A massage with 180-degree views awaits at the glass-walled fitness center and spa, where nine treatment rooms and private "relaxation pods" are set on the hotel's 10th-floor rooftop level.

Hamilton Place, Park Lane; 800/332-3442 or 44-20/7499-0888; fourseasons.com; doubles from $$$$.

45 Park Lane's lobby lounge.

Four Seasons Hotel London at Park Lane's Grand Suite.

An Xpanded riverside suite
at LX Boutique Hotel.

LISBON

LX BOUTIQUE HOTEL

CONSIDER THE LX BOUTIQUE HOTEL A window into Lisboan culture. Once a watering hole catering to the local literati in the laid-back Cais do Sodré area, the building has been reborn as a sophisticated inn that puts traditional elements of Portuguese identity at the forefront. The 45 blue-tinged rooms call to mind the nearby Tagus River as well as the country's vibrant *azulejo* tiles. Rooms come in three quirky sizes: Xssential, Xpanded, and Xplendid. Every level takes inspiration from a different historical cue, from the fifth-floor Bairro Alto—where murals of cobblestoned streets pay homage to Lisbon's most fashionable neighborhood—to the second-floor Fernando Pessoa, named for the 20th-century poet who penned some of his work at the property. Once dusk approaches, candles line the stairwell that takes you toward the Fado floor, casting shadows as hauntingly romantic as the music itself.

12 Rua do Alecrim; 351/213-474-394; lxboutiquehotel.com; doubles from $.

The hotel's cerulean façade. Below: A view of the Tagus River from an Xplendid suite.

L'AND VINEYARDS

IT USED TO BE THAT PORTUGAL'S wine-making tradition hinged more on the country's cork oaks than on its grapes. But in the eastern hills of the Alentejo—a region of sleepy villages, deserted castles, and roadside sheep just 60 miles from Lisbon—a slow yet steady evolution is under way. To experience it firsthand, book a room at L'And Vineyards, a modern hideaway where wine is hardly an afterthought. In addition to an outdoor lounge with 40 offerings by the glass, the on-site winery hosts daily enology classes and the Caudalie vinotherapy spa and hammam incorporate antioxidant-rich grape seeds and skins in treatments. After the nightly tasting, kick back in one of the resort's 22 concrete-and-wood villas; the best is the Sky View Suite, which has a fully retractable ceiling for stargazing.

4 Estrada Nacional; 351/266-242-400; l-andvineyards.com; doubles from $$.

The indoor pool
overlooking the garden
at L'And Vineyards.

VILLABUENA DE ÁLAVA, SPAIN

HOTEL VIURA

ANYONE WHO KNOWS THEIR GEHRY from their Calatrava
can tell you: architectural marvels flourish in Rioja, Spain's
northern wine region. In the little-known village of Villabuena
de Álava, there's now one more. The surreal Hotel Viura—
conceived by Spanish firm Designhouses and named for
the area's most widely planted grape—rises from the rustic
landscape like a Modernist mirage. Glass-and-reinforced-
concrete cubes are stacked on top of one another like off-kilter
building blocks; inside, exposed concrete walls play off a spare
cream-and-white palette. This being wine country, the staff
can arrange for outings to the surrounding vineyards, though
you can just as easily sample the goods from the hotel's cellar,
which holds more than 200 bins of local bottles. Sip them
in the restaurant, where golden barrels hover overhead, or at
the rooftop lounge, with their provenance spread out for
miles in the distance.

Calle Mayor; 34/94-560-9000; hotelviura.com; doubles from $.

The cubic structures that house Hotel Viura.

Wine barrels as design motif at the hotel's restaurant. Below: A Viura guest room.

BARCELONA
BARCELÓ RAVAL

FOR MUCH OF ITS HISTORY, EL RAVAL WAS A CROSS between Montmartre and the pre-Giuliani Times Square: a seedy district of brothels and petty crime. Now it's one of Barcelona's hottest neighborhoods—thanks in part to the sleek Barceló Raval hotel, set in a striking cylindrical tower wrapped in black-metal mesh. Public spaces brim with playful elements, from a life-size horse lamp to a table made in the likeness of a wild boar. Hot-pink headboard lighting offsets the minimalist vibe in the guest rooms, where floor-to-ceiling windows are draped in thick black fabric to keep the city glare at bay. Upstairs, a rooftop bar offers unparalleled 360-degree vistas of Las Ramblas, the Barri Gòtic, and beyond. If you prefer to see the sights at eye level, Plaza de Catalunya and the Museu d'Art Contemporani de Barcelona are just a few blocks away.

17-21 Rambla del Raval; 34/93-320-1490; barceloraval.com; doubles from $.

Barceló Raval's
B-Lounge restaurant.

Gauzy curtains outside a Cap Rocat suite. Below: The room's ikat-draped four-poster bed.

The Fortress patio lounge at Cap Rocat.

CALA BLAVA, SPAIN

CAP ROCAT

WITH ITS PREENING SUMMER CROWDS AND THROBBING NIGHTLIFE, Majorca attracts almost too much attention for some. If you're looking to go off the radar, retreat over the drawbridge from Palma to the crenellated Cap Rocat, in a 19th-century military fortress along the southern edge of the Bay of Palma. The hotel takes its cues from the structure's soldierly past with suites set in former munitions stores and door handles fashioned from stylized bullets. Yet a relaxed air of privilege prevails: armchairs swathed in rich striped fabrics; handsome teak shutters; soothing exposed-limestone walls. The grounds, too, are a study in elegance, with rows of manicured topiaries and all-weather canopy beds on the terraces. The scene stealer, however, has to be the saltwater infinity pool, a watering hole that looks like an extension of the Mediterranean.

Crta. de Cap Enderrocat; 34/97-174-7878; caprocat.com; doubles from $$$.

PYLA-SUR-MER, FRANCE

LA CO(O)RNICHE

FISHERMEN OUTNUMBER FASHIONISTAS
in the seaside enclave of Cap Ferret,
on France's rugged western coast. But
just across the cobalt-blue waters of
the Arcachon Basin, Philippe Starck's
trendy La Co(o)rniche hotel is dramatically
inverting that ratio. The mood in the
former hunting lodge is that of a stylish
summerhouse, one that has traded
rusticity for a whitewashed version of
the designer's urbane aesthetic. Twelve
sun-filled guest rooms have gray wood
floorboards and bead-board walls,
white-tiled baths, and beds in the center
of the room. Shelves are adorned with
well-worn accessories, from postcards
to aluminum sculptures that recall
the area's breezy history. The restaurant's
modern *cuisine de terroir* has the
basin buzzing each evening. That party
atmosphere is set to a slightly lower
volume at lunch—the best time to snag
a poolside table and gaze out at the
paragliders hovering like butterflies over
the nearby dunes.

46 Ave. Louis Gaume; 33-5/56-22-72-11;
lacoorniche-pyla.com; doubles from $$.

The infinity pool
overlooking
the Arcachon Basin.
Above: Salmon
carpaccio in
the restaurant.

europe

119

Thierry Marx's
Camélia restaurant
at the Mandarin
Oriental, Paris.

PARIS

MANDARIN ORIENTAL

ON A FASHIONABLE STRETCH OF RUE ST.-HONORÉ, a magic carpet twinkling with fiber-optic lights transports guests from the street to a courtyard garden at the heart of a listed Art Deco building. This is the Mandarin Oriental, Paris, equal parts nightclub and nature preserve, with splashes of haute couture. The glamour of the entry continues in the modernist rooms and suites, where no detail—soundproof walls; international electrical outlets; an abstracted Man Ray photograph printed on velvet headboards—goes unchecked. True to the Mandarin Oriental brand, Asian touches appear throughout: miso soup on the room-service breakfast menu; *manga*-like silverleaf butterflies flitting across a white-glass mosaic in the spa. The restaurants, however—under the deft hand of legendary chef Thierry Marx—are unwaveringly French. And across the board, the company's much-touted service remains right on target—in other words, invisible.

251 Rue St.-Honoré, First Arr.; 800/526-6566 or 33-1/70-98-78-88; mandarinoriental.com; doubles from $$$$$.

PAVILLON DES LETTRES

VOLTAIRE, ZOLA, HUGO—literary roots run deep in the City of Light. That notion wasn't lost on the owners of the Pavillon des Lettres, a scribe-centric boutique hotel on a quiet side street steps from the Champs-Élysées. The 26 guest rooms (one for each letter of the alphabet) pay homage to some of the world's greatest authors, their prose papered on the walls and oeuvres lining the shelves. Didier Benderli, the protégé of French architect Jacques Garcia, has imbued the interiors with a masculine sexiness: dark velvet furnishings; stone floors; peekaboo glass-enclosed bathrooms. In-room iPads are programmed with daily news installments from *Le Figaro*. Book the top-floor Hans Christian Andersen Suite, with its reading nook overlooking the rooftops of the Faubourg St.-Honoré. Those inclined to follow the lead of the hotel's more decadent muses—Proust, Flaubert, Baudelaire— might opt instead for a drink at the diminutive bar.

12 Rue des Saussaies, Eighth Arr.; 33-1/49-24-26-26; pavillondeslettres.com; doubles from $$.

A junior suite at Pavillon des Lettres.

LE LAC DU PÊCHER, FRANCE

INSTANTS D'ABSOLU-ECOLODGE DU LAC DU PÊCHER

HIGH IN THE HILLS OF AUVERGNE, a five-hour drive south of Paris, Instants d'Absolu-Ecolodge isn't for those seeking high-tech amenities or over-the-top service. *Calme,* on the other hand, is to be had in abundance: the farmhouse is surrounded by miles of forested parkland, volcanic peaks, and a 40-acre alpine lake. Twelve simple guest rooms hew to an eco-friendly sensibility, which here means a pared-down Nordic vibe, with raw pine tables and rough-luxe fabrics such as alpaca, leather, and virgin wool. Uncannily soft pillows are made from recycled water bottles, while organic-cotton robes await in the lava-stone spa. Beyond the hotel grounds, outdoor activities abound, from trout fishing in the lake to snowshoeing through the woods. Afterward, restore yourself with a glass of locally distilled pine liqueur—the perfect aperitif before a dinner of duck with whiskey sauce and juniper berries, served in front of a roaring fire.

15300 Chavagnac, Cantal; 33-4/71-20-83-09; ecolodge-france.com; doubles from $.

Instants d'Absolu-Ecolodge's outdoor hot tub, overlooking Pêcher Lake.

Armani/Ristorante at Armani Hotel Milano. Above: The hotel's Presidential Suite.

ARMANI HOTEL MILANO

GIORGIO ARMANI knows how to make headlines for more than the exquisite garments he sends down fashion week runways each year. The designer's buzz-worthy stint in the hospitality industry began at Dubai's record-breaking 162-story Burj Khalifa in 2010. More recently, he's set his sights closer to home, opening the impressive Armani Hotel Milano above his flagship store in the Italian fashion capital. A fitting example of Armani's trademark brand of understated chic, the 95 spacious rooms resemble subdued jewel boxes filled with gold and cream upholstery and streamlined custom furniture. His taste for Asian-inspired simplicity shines through in the marble baths and the glass-enclosed Bamboo Bar on the top floor. Here, guests can dine under 23-foot ceilings while admiring a 360-degree panorama of Milan—Armani's tribute to the city he adores.

31 Via Manzoni; 39-02/8883-8888; armanihotels.com; doubles from $$$.

A guest room terrace edged in bamboo plants.

VENICE

VENISSA RISTORANTE OSTELLO

FOODIES WON'T MIND VENTURING OFF Venice's beaten path to reach the Venissa Ristorante Ostello, a no-fuss restaurant-inn on remote Mazzorbo island, 40 minutes by vaporetto from Piazza San Marco. Six understated rooms mix rustic elements such as wooden rafters and vintage wardrobes with Italian haute design (colorful Driade rugs; light fixtures by Artemide). Extras are virtually nonexistent—there's no spa or mini-bars—but it's a small price to pay when you have Paola Budel in the kitchen downstairs. Revered among Italy's top toques for her experimental palate, the former executive chef of Milan's Hotel Principe di Savoia serves innovative dishes like pan-fried eel with broccoli cream made using ingredients from Venissa's gardens and the lagoon just steps away. Make reservations now, though: tables fill up as quickly as you might expect.

3 Fondamenta Santa Caterina; 39-041/527-2281; venissa.it; doubles from $.

The outdoor dining patio at Venissa Ristorante Ostello.

The lobby lounge at the St. Regis Florence.

FLORENCE

ST. REGIS

ST. REGIS SPARED NO EXPENSE for its first hotel in the Renaissance capital. The company chose a 15th-century palazzo designed by Duomo architect Filippo Brunelleschi, the former site of the Grand Hotel. It took three years for permits to go through, but the result was worth the wait. Butler service is a given, and guests can bank on opulence at every turn: many of the 100 rooms fly the Medici-inspired flag of silks and velvets in royal and ecclesiastical shades. There's also Etichetta Pinchiorri, a restaurant by the team behind Florence's Michelin three-starred Enoteca Pinchiorri. In homage to the city's heritage, Florentine artisans were hired to restore frescoes and create patterned leather panels in the public spaces. Gilded mirrors and antiques are peppered throughout. It's as close as you can get to sleeping in the Uffizi Gallery—legally, that is.

1 Piazza d'Ognissanti; 877/787-3447 or 39-055/27161; stregis.com; doubles from $$.

The Mediterranean-facing infinity pool at Capo-Spartivento Lighthouse.

SARDINIA, ITALY

CAPO-SPARTIVENTO LIGHTHOUSE

NINE DAYS IN CAGLIARI was all it took to spur D. H. Lawrence to write one of the last century's great travel narratives, *Sea and Sardinia*. Spend a night at the Capo-Spartivento Lighthouse—on an isolated promontory at the island's southernmost tip—and you may be inspired to pen a classic of your own. The 1856 lighthouse maintains an official role for the Italian Navy, which still operates its third-story lantern. As for the floors below, owner Alessio Raggio has filled the four barrel-vaulted brick guest rooms with Murano-glass chandeliers and worldly wood furnishings (Indian mirrors; a Moroccan screen) while adding eco-friendly touches such as water-heating solar panels. Glass ceilings in two garden "apartments" provide an unobstructed view of the constellations, as does the glass-enclosed restaurant, which serves just-caught fish cooked to order. A cellar in a former cistern brims with bottles of Sardinian wine ripe for the picking.

Chia; no phone; farocapospartivento.com; doubles from $$$, including breakfast.

CAPRI, ITALY

CAPRI TIBERIO PALACE

WHEN THE EUROPEAN GLITTERATI fly south for the summer, one of their top stops is the endlessly chic Capri Tiberio Palace, a 19th-century landmark on the lemon-scented isle. Fashion designer turned architect Giampiero Panepinto's soothing pastel-hued interiors call to mind the mod motifs of the 1960's in polka-dot chairs and inlaid majolica floors. The sparkling waters of the Mediterranean, which can be seen from most of the 58 spacious guest rooms, lend their own inspiration; a rocky beach is just a short walk away. If you're inclined to stay put, the mosaic-lined indoor-outdoor pool offers cool comfort, and the spa is stocked with Sodashi products. Dishes such as house-made linguine with shrimp and baby zucchini play a starring role at the ever-packed Terrazza Tiberio restaurant. Afterward, order the signature Princess cocktail at the Jacky bar— a Cotton Club redux by way of Cuba.

11-15 Via Croce; 39-081/978-7111; capritiberio palace.com; doubles from $$$.

The barrel-vaulted Terrace Suite, overlooking the Mediterranean.

SAVELLETRI DI FASANO, ITALY

BORGO EGNAZIA

AT FIRST GLANCE, you might mistake the new Borgo Egnazia for one of the ancient fortified farmhouses that dot the countryside. Indeed, the white stone monolith is a paean to traditional Pugliese residences. With the Adriatic unfolding before it and poppies and silvery olive trees at every angle, the resort's 40 acres are split among a village-style complex of 92 town-house suites, 28 three-bedroom villas with private pools and gardens, and 63 bleached rooms in a boutique-style main building. Accommodations join luxe amenities—limestone double sinks; shaded terraces—with unexpected design moments (single olive branches in lieu of flowers). Twin pools are huge and lounge-worthy. The on-site cooking school takes advantage of the local bounty; the same goes for the hotel's four restaurants. Of course, no Italian hideaway would be complete without a low-key pizza joint: try the pie with fresh *burrata* cheese and *capocollo* ham.

Puglia; 39-080/225-5000; borgoegnazia.com; doubles from $$$.

A view of the Adriatic Sea beyond Borgo Egnazia's grounds.

AMSTERDAM

TOURISTS HAVE LONG FLOCKED TO THE San Francisco of Europe for its charming canals and famously tolerant social policies, but now the stylish hotel scene is attracting a new kind of visitor. These properties are helping redefine the Dutch capital.

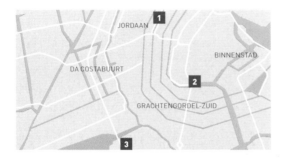

1 CANAL HOUSE

Spread across three 17th-century merchant's residences in the trendy Jordaan neighborhood, Canal House embodies the district's art-driven surroundings with a moody color palette (black walls in the bar; deep purple comforters) and fabrics (silk wallpaper) that recall traditional Dutch paintings. Historic references include original wood beams and fireplaces and decorative moldings.

ROOM TO BOOK Splurge on one of the Great rooms for the king-size bed and double vanities; in addition to mini-bars stocked with locally sourced treats, many offer views of the Keizersgracht. **DON'T MISS** Order a house-made Dutch apple pie with Chantilly cream in the light-filled Great Room restaurant, which overlooks the hotel's unusually large (for Amsterdam) flower gardens.

148-152 Keizersgracht; 31-20/622-5182; canalhouse.nl; doubles from $$.

Canal House's Exceptional Room.

② HOTEL DE L'EUROPE

From its perch on the Amstel River, the iconic Hotel de L'Europe has reemerged from a two-year renovation with all the grandeur of a royal palace. Built on the site of a 14th-century tower, the 1896 hotel is home to a smoking room with a walk-in humidor, as well as four Euro-chic restaurants. Soon to come: a state-of-the-art spa and wellness center. **ROOM TO BOOK** The 23 loftlike suites in the new Dutch Masters Wing feature paintings inspired by those in the Rijksmuseum, the city's premier art and history museum, plus motion-activated lighting and heated floors. **DON'T MISS** Les Caves de L'Europe, the hotel's 1,000-bottle-strong wine cellar, now hosts guided tours, tastings, and seminars on sommelier Dannis Apeldoorn's indigenous and far-flung selections.

2-8 Nieuwe Doelenstraat; 31-20/531-1777; leurope.nl; doubles from $$.

③ CONSERVATORIUM HOTEL

A newcomer on the hotel scene is the elegant Conservatorium Hotel, in an 1897 Renaissance Revival building. With interiors designed by Milanese architect Piero Lissoni, the 129-room property pays homage to its music conservatory roots in the atrium-style lobby and bar, which flanks the structure's original brick courtyard. **ROOM TO BOOK** Duplex Superior suites provide separate spaces for sleep and play, with bedrooms in the loft and streamlined Danish Modern furniture below; they also have windows facing the famed Museumplein. **DON'T MISS** The 10,000-square-foot Akasha spa's treatment rooms are inspired by the four elements—fire, water, air, and earth. There's also a heated Watsu pool and designated areas for yoga and tai chi.

27 Van Baerlestraat; 31-20/670-1811; conservatoriumhotel.com; doubles from $$$.

The Brasserie Hoofdstad restaurant in Hotel de L'Europe.

An atmospheric Duplex Superior suite at the Conservatorium Hotel.

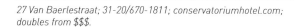

The kid-friendly
Club Room at
25hours Hotel
HafenCity.

The L-Bette Suite.
Above: A conference
room that incorporates
shipping containers.

25HOURS HOTEL HAFENCITY

DON'T BE FOOLED by the austere red-brick façade. There's an insouciant informality to the 25hours Hotel HafenCity, in Hamburg's docklands district. For inspiration, its designers eschewed Teutonic restraint and instead looked to the enclave's maritime roots. The 170 guest "cabins" are rife with nautical accents such as porthole-style mirrors and pilot ladder shelving; the lobby's concrete walls are adorned with massive ship propellers; and the check-in area resembles nothing so much as a boat loading dock. These days, the harborfront demographic is less about sea-worn sailors than cutting-edge creative types, who gather at the glass-walled Heimat Küche & Bar for lamb bratwurst and local lagers, practice their DJ skills in the Vinyl Room, or relax in the rooftop sauna. Should they share the same roving spirit, however, a fleet of bicycles and Mini Coopers is available free of charge.

5 Überseeallee; 49-40/226-229-590; 25hours-hotels.com; doubles from $.

europe

135

An extra-large
guest room at Soho
House Berlin.

BERLIN

SOHO HOUSE

REINVENTION IS AN OVERRIDING THEME
in modern-day Berlin, so it's fitting
that the local outpost of London's Soho
House—bordering the über-hip Mitte and
Prenzlauer Berg neighborhoods—has an
especially rich past: the 1920's Bauhaus
building has housed both a famous Jewish
department store *and* the Communist
Party archives. These days, it is an unlikely
dose of English eccentricity that has
transformed the raw-concrete interiors:
Damien Hirst artworks; retro floral
upholstery; Ping-Pong tables in the lobby.
At the 30-seat movie theater you can sink
into red velvet armchairs and watch classic
films. The 40 guest rooms are equally
homey, with luxe faux-fur comforters,
Midcentury antiques, and heated bathroom
floors. The Cowshed spa's Turkish bath
adds a touch of exoticism. Of course, no
one should miss a dip in the rooftop pool—
come summer, the coolest spot in town.

*1 Torstrasse; 49-30/405-0440; sohohouseberlin.com;
doubles from $$.*

europe

137

The Nobis Suite at
Nobis Hotel. Left:
A golden chandelier
by Gunnar Syrén
in the Lounge.

NOBIS HOTEL

THOUGH ITS COLOR PALETTE DRAWS from the stark Nordic winter—slate
grays, deep browns, icy whites—the newest hotel in Stockholm's central
square is as warm and convivial as it gets. Celebrated Sweden-based
firm Claesson Koivisto Rune opted for airiness in the public spaces:
witness the Lounge, a magnificent atrium where the city's beau monde
congregates for drinks under a 91-foot-high frescoed ceiling. In the
rooms, accents such as felt poufs and marble-topped coffee tables
exude a sense of calm to match the natural light streaming in. A worthy
splurge: the wood-paneled Nobis Suite, with its massive canopy
bed and 19th-century stucco detailing. By nightfall, scenesters jockey
for position at Caina, the hotel's rustic Italian restaurant, and at the
sleek Gold Bar, where legendary mixologist Robby Radovic oversees the
cocktail queue. The drinks may be cold, but the atmosphere is white-hot.

2-4 Norrmalmstorg; 46-8/614-1010; nobishotel.com; doubles from $$.

A sitting area
near the mirrored
reception desk.

A view of Aman
Sveti Stefan from
the mainland.

SVETI STEFAN, MONTENEGRO

AMAN SVETI STEFAN

ON THE SURFACE, the UNESCO-protected island of Sveti Stefan seems like a land out of time: a cluster of 15th-century stone cottages rising from a rocky outcropping in the Adriatic, connected to the mainland by a pink-sand isthmus. Look closer, though, and you'll find contemporary updates throughout—the result of a multimillion-dollar makeover by the Singapore-based luxury hotel group Amanresorts. That translates to 50 spacious suites that play on traditional Dalmatian interiors with fluid lines, wood-beamed ceilings, and soothing white stone walls. The village-resort also took over a former royal palace on the mainland— the eight-suite Villa Miločer—where dinner is served on a wisteria-fringed loggia to the sound of waves lapping the beach. For an authentic experience of Montenegrin life, head to the piazza—a square lined with restaurants, shops, and an immaculately restored church— and join the residents for glasses of Vranac, the local red, and regional specialties like *njeguski prsut* (a delicately flavored ham).

800/477-9180 or 382-33/420-000; amanresorts.com; doubles from $$$$.

The Karagiozis Suite
at the New Hotel.

ATHENS

NEW HOTEL

ONE OF THE WORLD'S OLDEST CITIES is getting a serious dose of high style. While the 79-room New Hotel nods to classical Greek motifs (Karagiozis shadow puppets; evil-eye wall installations), this interpretation is thoroughly up-to-date. Working with students from the University of Thessaly, avant-garde Brazilian designers Fernando and Humberto Campana—noted pioneers of sustainable chic— have repurposed items that are as sumptuous as they are environ- mentally friendly: bamboo-parquet floors, brass-clad washbasins, and workbenches forged from recycled materials. Original details, including the black marble staircase in the lobby, offset chairs handmade from broken furniture parts; the pieces were also used to create a kind of arbor in the ground-floor restaurant. The result is a striking counterpoint to Athens's most widely referenced symbol of all, the Acropolis, located mere blocks from the hotel's front door.

16 Fillellinon St.; 800/337-4685; newhotel.gr; doubles from $.

An alfresco lobby
at the Romanos.

MESSENIA, GREECE

THE ROMANOS, A LUXURY COLLECTION RESORT

A ONETIME HAUNT OF HELLENIC ROYALTY, the Peloponnesian beaches of Messenia are in the throes of a second heyday. Experience them for yourself at the 321-room Romanos, the first of a four-resort development whose ethos is unexpectedly eco-minded: 80 percent of the hotel operates on solar power; the golf course is irrigated with rainwater; and a conservation office is dedicated to preserving the seafront community. Indulgence, however, still plays a pivotal role. A 43,000-square-foot spa employs olive oil–based treatments derived from tablets discovered at the 3,400-year-old Palace of Nestor nearby. The resort's 32 light-filled suites have private pools and marble baths. And the breakfast spread alone features five varieties of local honey.

Navarino Dunes, Costa Navarino; 800/325-3589 or 30-272/309-6000; romanoscostanavarino. com; doubles from $$.

europe

143

EDITION

WHEN HAUTE HOTELIER IAN SCHRAGER merged forces with hospitality giant Marriott International, many expected another too-cool boutique. But in the Turkish style capital, the result is the Edition, a hotel that favors comfort over ironic gestures and tongue-in-cheek design statements. There's still plenty of glamour: the lobby is awash in gold-leaf and silver travertine; a glowing aquarium occupies a full wall in one of the seating areas. It all serves as a prelude to the soothing cream-and-taupe linens, heavy silk drapery, and wood-grain walls of the 78 guest rooms. None of Schrager's properties are complete without a splashy new restaurant; here, award-winning Venetian fare comes courtesy of the legendary Cipriani. Everything is trumped, however, by the tri-level Espa spa, whose 20,000 square feet include an octagonal hammam and a snow-fringed cabin where you can cool off post-steam. Comfort, indeed.

136 Buyukdere Cad.; 800/466-9695 or 90-212/317-7700; editionhotels.com; doubles from $$.

Edition Istanbul's Rosewood Suite.

ST. PETERSBURG, RUSSIA

W

VISITORS NEED LOOK NO FURTHER than the W St. Petersburg for evidence of the city's latest style revival. Set in a rebuilt 19th-century residential structure near the Hermitage, the brand's first foray into Eastern Europe features 137 streamlined rooms with Fabergé-worthy details. Dappled light glints off lamps shaped like gilded disco balls; jewel-toned upholstered furniture and lace-textured headboards impart a feeling of luxury. Downstairs, another imaginative lighting choice (a chandelier made of gold chain metal) draws attention at Alain Ducasse's Mix in St. Petersburg. On the pool deck, it's the Antonio Citterio–designed armchairs that steal the spotlight. Come sunset—as late as 11:30 p.m. in summer—the rooftop Terrace bar best captures the buzzy zeitgeist.

6 Voznesensky Prospekt; 877/946-8357 or 7-812/610-6161; whotels.com; doubles from $$.

The view of St. Isaac's Cathedral from MixUp Bar at the W St. Petersburg.

Inside room No. 2
at Ngong House,
in Nairobi.

FEZMARRAKESHNAIROBILOITAHILLSTANZANIAZAMBIAS
ALKHAIMAHFEZMARRAKESHNAIROBILOITAHILLSTANZANIAZ

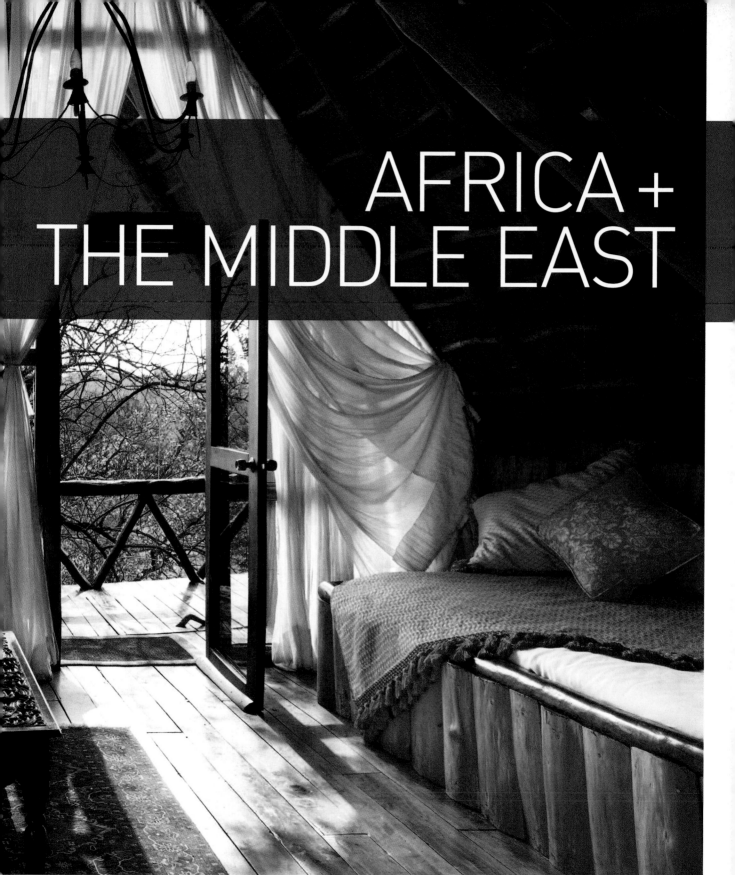

AFRICA +
THE MIDDLE EAST

THAFRICATELAVIVNEGEVDESERTSIRBANIYASDUBAIRAS
BIASOUTHAFRICATELAVIVNEGEVDESERTSIRBANIYASDUBAI

FEZ, MOROCCO

PALAIS AMANI

THE PACE OF LIFE IS DECIDEDLY SERENE behind the doors of the Palais Amani, a sophisticated haven in the heart of the medina. A 3½-year restoration has enhanced the existing features of the Art Deco–tinged *riad*—mosaic-adorned walls and floors; stained-glass windows; carved-wood doors—while adding such details as brass knockers, embroidered linens, and calligraphy from some of the most skilled artisans in town. Furnishings in the 14 rooms are spare, the better to play up those decorative flourishes. The souk is just steps away, but guests looking for quiet stimulation will find plenty of it here: steaming in the hammam, de-stressing with an aromatic massage under the rooftop pergola, or just sipping tea under fragrant citrus trees in the courtyard by the tiled fountain.

12 Derb El Miter, Oued Zhoune, Hay Blida; 212-535/633-209; palaisamani.com; doubles from $.

The fountain
in Palais Amani's
atrium garden.

The courtyard at Riad Joya Marrakech. Below: An antique hookah in the Living Room lounge.

MARRAKESH, MOROCCO

RIAD JOYA MARRAKECH

SUBTLE NODS TO MOROCCAN DESIGN— those ubiquitous metal lanterns and *tadelakt* walls—look unexpectedly fresh at Riad Joya, in the medina's Mouassin quarter. A team of Italian owners created a pared-down sensibility in the seven sand-toned suites, each inspired by the city's varied historical influences: Zanzibar channels the African coast with ikat-patterned end tables and a bed edged in mosquito netting; Dar Arabe showcases Arab craftsmanship with its inlaid-wood furnishings and blown-glass lamps. Despite the property's small size, a large staff of butlers, drivers, and guides is on call for shopping excursions in the souk or day trips to the beach town of Essaouira. And when another *tagine* is one too many, head to the hotel's restaurant for surprisingly authentic Tuscan dishes like *risotto alle fave* (risotto with fava beans). The Moroccan chef trained, after all, with one of the owners' Italian *mammas*.

26-27 Hay Mouassine, Derb El Hammam; 212-524/391-624; riadjoya.com; doubles from $.

Traditional accents
in the subdued
Dar Arabe Suite.

NAIROBI

ADVENTURE-BOUND TRAVELERS ONCE considered the Kenyan capital a mere pit stop en route to a safari. But a burst of creativity in everything from fashion to the arts is establishing the city as a destination in its own right. The best hotels offer a mix of quintessentially urban experiences and dazzling, only-in-Africa landscapes.

1 TRIBE HOTEL

Not far from the U.S. Embassy in the heart of Gigiri, the 137-room Tribe Hotel looks like a W on safari, with pan-African sculptures in the lobby, tribal-print throws in the rooms, and modern furniture designed by local artists scattered throughout. Given its location, the hotel attracts an eclectic mix of hipsters and diplomats. Meanwhile, the restaurant Jiko has become a popular gathering spot for fashionable young Nairobians thanks to its organic farm-to-table specialties. **ROOM TO BOOK** Earth-toned Deluxe rooms have sandstone walls and hardwood floors and built-ins; opt for one with a freestanding tub. **DON'T MISS** You can sip alfresco cocktails and choose your own tobacco flavor at the hookah bar on the rooftop terrace, which overlooks the Diplomatic District.

Limuru Rd., Gigiri; 254-20/720-0000; tribe-hotel.com; doubles from $$.

Hand-embroidered linens at the Tribe Hotel.

2 SANKARA NAIROBI

The emerging Westlands neighborhood is home to the business-chic Sankara Nairobi, a 156-room hotel that combines Asian and African influences, from an Angsana spa by the Thailand wellness group Banyan Tree to a gallery of contemporary art by Kenyan painters. Another highlight: more than 1,000 bottles of wine line two glass-enclosed walls in the second-floor bar and delicatessen.

ROOM TO BOOK A glass partition separates bedrooms and bathrooms in Superior rooms; or splurge on one of the sixth-floor Club rooms, which provide access to an exclusive private lounge.

DON'T MISS On the hotel's roof, you can check out the view below from a glass-bottom pool set eight stories above the city or dine on tapas at the Sarabi Pool & Supper Club.

Woodvale Grove, Westlands; 254-20/420-8000; sankara.com; doubles from $$.

3 FAIRMONT THE NORFOLK

Since its opening, the 108-year-old Fairmont The Norfolk has been the city's most notable place to stay. The Tudor-style landmark's classically plush accommodations evoke the current millenium with marble vanities, walk-in closets, and velour carpeting in the 165 rooms. Newer additions include a wine bar with an adjacent bird-filled terrace and a steak house serving sustainably farmed Kenyan Angus beef. Outside, acres of tropical foliage provide a buffer from bustling downtown Nairobi.

ROOM TO BOOK The eight suites in the 1937 block feature courtyard views and private patios.

DON'T MISS Local teas, coffees, and traditional Kenyan sweets such as *mandazi* (doughnuts) are presented each afternoon in the sumptuous new Tea Room, outfitted with cozy patterned armchairs.

Harry Thuku Rd., Central Business District; 800/441-1414 or 254-20/226-5000; fairmont.com; doubles from $$.

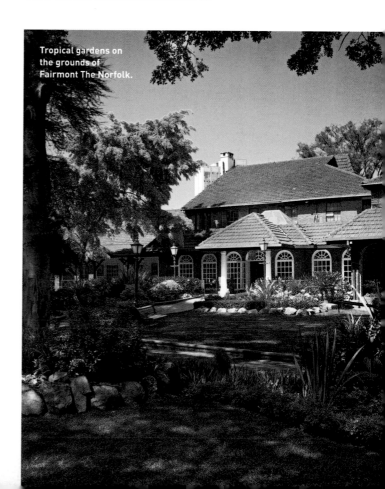

Sankara Nairobi's Sarabi Pool & Supper Club.

Tropical gardens on the grounds of Fairmont The Norfolk.

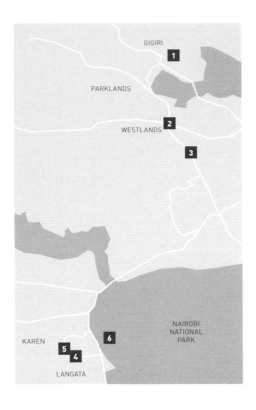

GIGIRI

1

PARKLANDS

2 WESTLANDS

3

NAIROBI
NATIONAL
PARK

KAREN 6

5 4

LANGATA

4 HOGMEAD

Near the genteel suburb of Karen, named for *Out of Africa* author Karen Blixen, Hogmead is run by the Safari & Conservation Company, which owns lodges throughout East Africa. The patrician country-house hotel's six bedrooms have stylish details such as wood-paneled soaking tubs and tribal-print pillows. Dinner and drinks are served on an open-air veranda warmed by a charcoal kiln on chilly evenings. At night, guests are serenaded by the sounds of bush babies and lions in the distance. **ROOM TO BOOK** The largest suite is Mara, with a private balcony and a seating area that looks out on the Ngong Hills. **DON'T MISS** The hotel is ideally situated for animal sightings. Warthog families wander the grounds and a 130-acre giraffe sanctuary and wildlife preserve borders the property.

Kikenni Rd., Langata; 254/712-579-9999; thesafariandconservation company.com; doubles from $$$$$.

The shaded entrance to Hogmead.

5 NGONG HOUSE

Down the road from Hogmead is Ngong House, an intimate tree-house-style boutique hotel on 10 acres of what was once Karen Blixen's coffee estate. With views of the hills that give the property its name, the six cottages are built on stilts and have quirky touches, such as knotty-wood bed frames, glass windows made of recycled bottles, African grass roofs, and bathtubs fashioned from Swahili canoes.

ROOM TO BOOK Families will appreciate the extra space in the rustic log cabin, which sleeps up to six people and has vaulted ceilings and a freestanding wood-burning fireplace.
DON'T MISS Costume designer Penny Winter sells her gemstone-studded necklaces and handmade caftans in a tiny shop next to the hotel's lobby; stop there after lunch, served under a canopy of acacia trees.

60 Ndovu Rd., Langata; 254/722-434-965; ngonghouse.com; doubles from $$$$, including breakfast and dinner.

6 NAIROBI TENTED CAMP

Now you can go on safari without leaving town: the eco-savvy Nairobi Tented Camp is set just west of the city center in a 28,800-acre park teeming with animals. Don't let the rugged environs fool you: luxury tents are furnished with sheepskin rugs, campaign-inspired wooden tables, and iron bed frames. The camp offers game drives and ranger-led walks, as well as tours of the nearby Kenya National Museum.

ROOM TO BOOK The eight canvas tents are practically identical, with private bathrooms and showers and small verandas lit by hurricane lamps.
DON'T MISS The park's inhabitants provide endless entertainment, whether you're observing lions and leopards stalking their prey; black and rare white rhinos cooling off by the local watering hole; or crowned eagles taking flight.

Nairobi National Park; 254/733-884-298; nairobitentedcamp.com; doubles from $$$, including meals.

A Swahili boat bathtub in room No. 7 at Ngong House.

Breakfast in Nairobi Tented Camp's central dining pavilion.

On the way
to Little Olarro's
Upper Lounge
dining deck,
overlooking the
Loita Hills.

A pool area at the lodge. Left: The villa's master bedroom.

LOITA HILLS, KENYA

OLARRO

THIS HILLSIDE LODGE ON THE EDGE OF THE MASAI MARA is fast becoming Kenya's next high-profile hideaway. Designer Anthony Russell brought the outdoors into the two-bedroom villa and seven thatched cottages: slate-tiled floors resemble giraffe markings, chairs are upholstered in animal-print textiles, and billowing fabric ceilings give the feel of a tented camp without the hassle of zippered doors. During the day, there's no better place to take in the annual wildebeest migration than from the basket of a hot-air balloon. Evening game drives involving elephant, leopard, and hyena sightings end with a lantern-lit bush dinner of *kuku choma* (chicken roasted over coals). And the ride back comes with a bonus: night-vision goggles that allow you to spot wildlife in the dark.

Masai Mara National Reserve; 263-13/42527; olarrokenya.com; doubles from $$$ per person, including meals.

SINGITA EXPLORE

SINGITA NEEDS NO INTRODUCTION among the safari set. South Africa's pioneering eco-tourism group made waves in the early 2000's with a series of ultra-luxe lodges in the Grumeti Reserve, 340,000 untouched acres in Tanzania's western Serengeti. Now the company is one-upping itself with a new mobile concept that allows guests to stay in the reserve's most remote areas without disturbing the zebras, impalas, and giraffes that congregate practically at your doorstep. Despite this rugged isolation, the vibe is unmistakably luxurious. Six canvas residences are modeled on early-20th-century-style encampments and accessorized with mahogany chests, utilitarian furniture, and raw felt rugs. Further proof that you're not exactly roughing it: after viewing lions and aardwolves with your private guide, you can sample gourmet takes on oxtail *potjie* (stew) and chocolate Malva pudding (a South African caramelized cake), all cooked over an open campfire.

Singita Grumeti Reserve; 770/852-6623 or 255-28/262-2071; singita.com; doubles from $$$$$ per person, all-inclusive.

A guest tent at
Singita Explore.

A lantern-lit
dinner table at
Manyara Ranch
Conservancy.

ARUSHA, TANZANIA

MANYARA RANCH CONSERVANCY

SET AMID THE BROAD SAVANNAS and acacia forests of northern Tanzania, Manyara attracts guests who want to see habitat restoration at work without sacrificing creature comforts. The private 35,000-acre former cattle ranch, home to a lion pride and hundreds of elephants, also serves as a pilot program for educating the local Masai on wildlife management. Unlike at many safari lodges, you can choose your own adventure: day or night drives, horseback rides, afternoons spent shadowing conservationists, and visits to the neighboring villages. The six extra-large tents have private decks, armchairs, and en suite bathrooms. A busy kitchen tent turns out picnic lunches. Evening meals are served alfresco after a round of sundowners at water's edge, mere feet away from elephants quenching their thirst.

255-27/254-5284; manyararanch.com; doubles from $$$ per person, all-inclusive.

SOUTH LUANGWA NATIONAL PARK, ZAMBIA

SANCTUARY ZEBRA PLAINS

DON'T EXPECT GAME DRIVES HERE. South Luangwa National Park is the birthplace of the walking safari, and Sanctuary Zebra Plains caters to the active set with trips spent exploring the park almost exclusively on foot. Guides take groups on twice-daily treks through the bush, accompanied by a traditional "tea bearer" who serves steaming cups of chai or coffee. Among the memorable sights: an island accessed via canoe and the Changwa Channel, which has one of the highest concentrations of hippos in the world. Visitors might also spot leopards and Thornicroft's giraffe, known for its distinctive star- and leaf-shaped markings. Back at camp, located on a wide sandbank at the juncture of two rivers, four canvas tents are decked out with vintage campaign furniture and the requisite mosquito netting. During breakfast, your nearest companion might just be a rare sable antelope—you're that close.

27-11/438-4650; sanctuaryretreats.com; doubles from $$$ per person, all-inclusive.

A tented bedroom at
Sanctuary Zebra Plains.

Babylonstoren's central fruit and vegetable gardens.

Inside a restored *landhuis*. Right: An entrance to the hotel's working farm.

BABYLONSTOREN

EVERY AFRIKANER FARM WORTH ITS SALT has a vegetable garden at its heart. And Babylonstoren, a 1777 Dutch homestead in the Cape Winelands, is no different. Little at the estate has changed since the 18th century, except that visitors are now welcome to stay within its stylishly redone walls. Traditional *landhuisies* (cottages) combine Boer austerity and the cool minimalism of a Philippe Starck-style abode, with Victorian-inspired claw-foot tubs and white sofas and rugs. Food lovers will want to book a room with a full kitchen—they face the eight-acre garden from which you can pick your own produce (the same used down the road in the restaurant Babel). Guided tours offer a closer look at the verdant centerpiece: a botanical library of more than 300 edible plants inspired in part by the mythical Hanging Gardens of Babylon. Consider it the ultimate farm-to-table fantasy.

Klapmuts Rd.; 27-21/863-3852; babylonstoren.com; doubles from $$$.

africa + the middle east

163

DELAIRE GRAFF LODGES & SPA

BRITISH DIAMOND JEWELER LAURENCE GRAFF is bringing some serious dazzle to the Cape Winelands, courtesy of this sprawling 10-lodge estate. At first glance, the hotel may seem like a cosmopolitan mash-up. Freestanding suites decorated by London interiors guru David Collins feature butlers' kitchens and plunge pools; peach-pit-and-red-resin floors in the supper club put a glossy spin on Afrikaner residences; and Graff's enviable art collection, including a William Kentridge portrait and bronze pieces by local sculptor Dylan Lewis, is on display throughout. But there's a distinctive regional pride at work as well. At the estate's two restaurants, Christiaan Campbell—one of the country's top chefs—draws from the area's bounty of ingredients for his pickled beetroot carpaccio with goat-cheese fritters and crayfish lasagna with king oyster mushrooms. The glass-walled wine cellar in the lobby is the perfect showcase for Delaire's award-winning vintages, made from grapes grown in the fields outside.

Rte. 310, Helshoogte Pass; 27-21/885-8160; delaire.co.za; doubles from $$$$$.

The slate Presidential Lodge at Delaire Graff Lodges & Spa.

BROWN HOTEL

LAST YEAR, THE ISRAELI HOTEL on everyone's lips was Jerusalem's white-on-white Mamilla. This year it's the Brown, a Tel Aviv boutique property that evokes a 1970's clubhouse thanks to soft lighting, earth tones (hence the name), and cordovan-leather couches. Centrally located a short walk from the beach and in sight of the fashionable Neve Tzedek quarter, the 30 guest rooms combine moody chocolate walls, crisp white sheets, and black-marble showers. Hallways feature works by local street artist Pilpeled, adding a dose of urban grit. On the roof deck, the view extends from the Bauhaus towers of the "White City," a collection of structures built in the 1930's, to the tranquil waters of the Mediterranean. It's just the place to start your night, cocktail in hand.

25 Kalisher St.; 972-3/717-0200; browntlv.com; doubles from $$.

The Brown Hotel's
rooftop deck.

A Desert View room with a pool at Beresheet.

MITZPE RAMON, ISRAEL

BERESHEET

IN A NATION OF WONDERS both natural and historic, Israel's 200 million-year-old Ramon Crater is a standout. Set in the stark Negev desert, 2½ hours south of Tel Aviv, the 23-mile-long geological depression is rich in rare wildlife and archaeological remnants from its first human inhabitants. Named after the Hebrew word for *genesis,* Beresheet more than lives up to its weighty moniker. Forty low-slung structures made of indigenous stone and tropical woods face the 1,000-foot-deep crater, where jeeps take visitors to see prehistoric fossils, early dwellings, and endangered birds and mammals. A dip in the crater-front pool is obligatory—what better way to drink in the desert than from a water-filled oasis?

Negev Desert; 972-8/659-8000; luxury-hotels-israel.com; doubles from $$.

SIR BANI YAS, UNITED ARAB EMIRATES

DESERT ISLANDS RESORT & SPA BY ANANTARA

THE ACTION OF ABU DHABI, 150 miles to the east, is replaced by the lull of waves on the eight Arabian Gulf atolls known as the Desert Islands. Only two of the archipelago's isles are inhabited, including Sir Bani Yas, home to the Desert Islands Resort & Spa by Anantara. The pristine natural setting is undeniably the draw, best observed on a hike to salt-dome hilltops or a game drive through the nearby Arabian Wildlife Park. The 64 Arabian-chic rooms provide respite from the heat, as do the kidney-shaped infinity pool and the beachfront spa; personal butlers in six villas take relaxation to the next level. Our favorite touch: in an effort to counter the effects of tourism, the resort plants a mangrove for each arriving guest.

971-2/801-5400; anantara.com; doubles from $$.

The pool area
at Desert Islands
Resort & Spa.

A sprawling Beach villa at
One&Only The Palm.

ONE&ONLY THE PALM

IN TRUE DUBAI FASHION, everything is over the top at the ultra-luxe One&Only The Palm, located on the man-made extravaganza of the Palm Jumeirah, in the Arabian Sea. There are Moorish-style buildings, Andalusian-inspired gardens, and multiple fountains along a white-sand shore, plus a 26,000-square-foot spa; French chef Yannick Alléno consults on the hotel's three restaurants. A free kids' club arranges activities with a cultural twist, from belly dancing to camping under the stars. Excursions for adults are equally exotic. Sand skiing or a camel caravan? A dhow cruise or a night at the races? Anything seems possible.

West Crescent; 866/552-0001 or 971-4/440-1010; oneandonlyresorts.com;
doubles from $$$$$.

High-backed seating in the hotel's entrance foyer.

171

A luxe daybed at
Banyan Tree Al Wadi's
Al Khaimah Villa.

BANYAN TREE AL WADI

SKYSCRAPERS AND DESIGNER SHOPS notwithstanding, much of the U.A.E. is actually desert, where sand dunes ripple toward a cobalt horizon. A 45-minute drive from Dubai, the Banyan Tree Al Wadi appears like a bedouin-style mirage— one with tented pavilions tucked into the honey-colored landscape. The 101 villas, each of which has its own infinity pool, blend lattice-wood panels and Arab-inspired carvings with Far East– style service (the spa specializes in Thai massage). More than half of the resort's 250 acres serve as a nature preserve, so you might spot wild gazelles from the restaurant's floor-to-ceiling windows. Yearning for your *Lawrence of Arabia* moment? Guides are on hand to lead camel expeditions into the dunes for vistas as burnt as the beating sun.

Al Mazraa; 800/591-0439 or 971-720/67777; banyantree.com; doubles from $$$.

africa + the middle east

173

JAPANHONGKONGSHANGHAINEWDELHIHYDERABADMALDI
SINGAPOREINDONESIAJAPANHONGKONGSHANGHAINEWDEL

ASIA

Villas along Lamai Bay at
Banyan Tree Samui,
in Koh Samui, Thailand.

VIETNAMPHNOMPENHBANGKOKKOHSAMUIHUAHINPENANG
HYDERABADMALDIVESVIETNAMPHNOMPENHBANGKOKKOHSAMUI

A suite at Green Leaf Niseko Village. Above: The entrance to the resort.

HOKKAIDO, JAPAN

GREEN LEAF NISEKO VILLAGE

WINTER ENTHUSIASTS LOOKING to touch down on Hokkaido's world-famous powder won't find a softer landing than at Green Leaf Niseko Village. At the foot of Mount Annupuri, the property is a true ski-in, ski-out resort, with easy rentals, efficient lifts, and lessons from top-notch instructors. The Modernist lodge also has style in spades, thanks to a recent revamp by designer Alexandra Champalimaud that melds Eastern serenity and European sophistication. Common areas feature chesterfield sofas and cowhide-covered lounges, while in the guest rooms, landscapes by artist Soichiro Tomioka rival the hotel's own bucolic views. After a day spent trying out the plentiful tree-lined runs, head for a soak in the resort's fabled *onsen*—natural mineral waters bordered by boulders, pines, and graceful snowdrifts.

Higashiyama-onsen, Niseko-cho, Abuta-gun; thegreenleafhotel.com; doubles from $$, including breakfast and dinner.

The Green Leaf *onsen*, a natural mineral bath.

HONG KONG

HULLETT HOUSE

IN A CITY THAT CELEBRATES all things modern, the 10-suite Hullett House—
set within an 1881 building that once served as the headquarters of the maritime
police—gives an unexpected nod to the past. Under the insouciant eye of
restaurateur and owner David Yeo, the palatial rooms on the southern tip of
Kowloon's fashionable Tsim Sha Tsui district riff on different moments in Chinese
history, whether it's Hong Kong's rural origins (signaled by birdcages and
bamboo in the turquoise-walled Stanley Suite) or Mao's reign (the Pop-art Casam
features a triptych of the Chairman blowing bubble gum). In Loong Toh Yuen,
one of the hotel's five restaurants, Sze Fsi puts his own spin on regional
favorites. Not to miss: the Tai O fried rice, a classic dish from the fishing village
of the same name, served here with fresh grilled shrimp and crunchy roe.

2A Canton Rd., Kowloon; 852/3988-0000; hulletthouse.com; doubles from $$$.

Hand-painted walls depicting birds and bamboo in Hullett House's Stanley Suite.

Loong Toh Yuen restaurant. Below: Ming dynasty–inspired murals in the D'Aguilar Suite.

The ninth-floor lobby at the Ritz-Carlton, Hong Kong. Left: Business district views behind the Lounge & Bar.

HONG KONG

RITZ-CARLTON

CALL IT KING KONG. This 1,600-foot-tall juggernaut commands floors 102 to 118 of Kowloon's International Commerce Centre. Created by cutting-edge firms that include Singapore's LTW Designworks and Japan's Spin Design Studio and Wonderwall, the 312-room site gives your heart multiple opportunities to skip a beat, even if you're not acrophobic. Start with the ride from the ninth-floor reception desk to the main lobby— at 20 miles per hour, it's about five times faster than any elevator ascent you've ever experienced. The top-floor infinity pool has a ceiling of LCD monitors showing the sky outside; the Lounge & Bar features crystal fire pits; and the scene-setting bar (dubbed, appropriately enough, Ozone) is also the highest in the world. Yoga lovers, be warned: classes are held on an outdoor terrace on the dizzying 118th floor.

1 Austin Rd. W., Kowloon; 800/241-3333 or 852/2263-2263; ritzcarlton.com; doubles from $$$.

One of the hotel's 20
Premier Island suites.

SHANGHAI

WELCOME TO A CITY IN FLUX. SHANGHAI HAS mastered the art of real-time reinvention, best witnessed in the vertical expansion of enclaves like Pudong and the Bund. Amid the ultramodern emphasis, however, lies a deep reverence for history—a Deco flourish here, a colonial-era detail there— and this trio of stylish hotels is no exception.

1 WALDORF ASTORIA SHANGHAI ON THE BUND

Waldorf Astoria pulled out all the stops for its China debut, on the Bund. A newly built 252-room tower has unexpected modern comforts such as Japanese electric toilets. But it's the 1911 Baroque-Revival building (the former home of the Shanghai Club, a hangout for colonial-era gentlemen) that steals the spotlight. In the lobby, Sicilian-marble floors set the tone, and a restored steel birdcage elevator leads to 20 glamorous guest rooms.

ROOM TO BOOK Corner suites in the heritage Waldorf Club wing provide extra square footage and views north on the Bund. In the Tower, the best values are the city-facing rooms on the 10th floor or higher.

DON'T MISS Order a gin-based Zaza cocktail at the 110-foot, L-shaped mahogany Long Bar, modeled on the original in the old Shanghai Club.

2 Zhong Shan Dong Yi Rd.; 800/925-3673 or 86-21/6322-9988; waldorfastoria.com; doubles from $$$.

Waldorf Astoria Shanghai on the Bund's Waldorf Suite, in the heritage building.

2 RITZ-CARLTON SHANGHAI, PUDONG

Despite the sheer volume of distractions in the frenetic Pudong district, the luxury brand's second Shanghai property offers plenty of reasons to stay put: four restaurants, a vertigo-inducing spa, and a rooftop bar. Topping off Cesar Pelli's 58-story IFC Shanghai building, the 285-room hotel pays homage to the area's Art Deco architecture with interiors by designer Richard Farnell that include fan-shaped chairs, mosaic-glass mirrors, and ornamental brass screens.

ROOM TO BOOK Opt for the Shanghai Bund View Suite for uninterrupted vistas of the waterfront and 24-hour Club Lounge access.

DON'T MISS Pamper yourself with an hour-long ginger-and-jasmine foot massage at the spa, on the hotel's 55th floor; then take the elevator three levels up and marvel at the skyline from an outdoor seat at Flair bar.

8 Century Ave.; 800/241-3333 or 86-21/2020-1888; ritzcarlton.com; doubles from $$$.

3 WATERHOUSE AT SOUTH BUND

In a once-abandoned 1930's warehouse on the southern Bund, the Waterhouse is a sleek departure from the high-rise hotels that light up the city center. Its postindustrial look begins in the austere lobby— exposed brick walls; steel beams; stone floors—and continues through guest quarters that blend rough concrete ceilings with blond-wood floors.

ROOM TO BOOK The Bund Junior Suite is known for its wide river views. Guests with voyeuristic tendencies might appreciate room No. 12, which features a glass shaftway that allows you to peer into a portion of the room below.

DON'T MISS At Table No. 1, Gordon Ramsay apprentice Jason Atherton consults on the seasonal, organic European fare, which is served in a minimalist dining room with several long communal tables.

No. 1-3 Bldg., Maojiayuan Rd.; 800/337-4685 or 86-21/6080-2988; waterhouseshanghai.com; doubles from $.

The gilded reception desk at the Ritz-Carlton Shanghai, Pudong.

Waterhouse at South Bund's rooftop terrace bar, with a view of Pudong.

The reflection pool outside Oberoi, Gurgaon's lobby.

NEW DELHI, INDIA

OBEROI, GURGAON

JUST OUTSIDE DOWNTOWN NEW DELHI in the newly minted financial capital of Gurgaon, the nine-acre Oberoi conveys an oasis-like calm, beginning with an entrance path that winds its way through a small forest and around a private lake. In the lobby, where sunlight streams in through floor-to-ceiling glass, a 10,000-square-foot vertical garden cascades to a reflecting pool lit with fire torches. Rooms, starting at 620 square feet, are some of the country's largest. There's no shortage of on-site amenities, including two restaurants, a 24-hour spa, a contemporary art gallery, and boutiques from such luxury labels as Bottega Veneta and Jimmy Choo. Still, it's the sense of serenity in one of India's economic boomtowns that makes this hotel a rare breed indeed.

443 Udyog Vihar, Gurgaon, Haryana; 800/562-3764 or 91-124/245-1234; oberoihotels.com; doubles from $$$.

LEELA PALACE

A PAIR OF CARVED-STONE ELEPHANTS marks the entrance to the Leela Palace New Delhi, which occupies a prominent perch near the foreign embassies in the city's Chanakyapuri district. But even non-diplomats have plenty of reasons to post themselves within its golden domes. The key here is service, which goes beyond the gentle *"namaste"* greeting and complimentary lemon-cranberry cocktails at check-in to accomplishing the near impossible (a middle-of-the-night phone call to change a morning flight). Each evening, guests are plied with platters of sweets such as the delectable *gulab jamun* (sugar-dusted fried dough coated in rosewater syrup); heartier sustenance, including lobster *neeruli*, is on offer at Jamavar, a glass box of a restaurant set in a tropical garden, where you can rub elbows with international ambassadors while you play dignitary for the day.

Diplomatic Enclave, Chanakyapuri; 800/323-7500 or 91-11/3933-1234; theleela.com; doubles from $$$.

The gilded dining room at Leela Palace New Delhi's Jamavar restaurant.

A carriage parked in front of Taj Falaknuma Palace's entrance.

HYDERABAD, INDIA

TAJ FALAKNUMA PALACE

LOOK NO FURTHER FOR a glamorous primer on the history of India's royal life. Crowning a hill high above town, this 1894 Palladian palace was once the residence of the city's nizam, or ruler, before it fell into disrepair. Now, fresh from a 10-year restoration, the white-marble building has become a living museum, complete with painstakingly revamped frescoes, Venetian chandeliers, and 60 opulent guest rooms done up in ivories and golds. Trade your car for a horse-drawn carriage at the gate, then ascend the steps as the staff showers you with rose petals. Wander the property if you like—nothing is off limits, whether that means playing pool in the embossed-leather billiard room or curling up in the mahogany-and-ebony-paneled library, whose collection of some 6,000 books includes rare editions of the Koran. Peacocks roam the regal grounds, which consist of original Moghul, Rajasthani, and Japanese gardens. The final touch to the fairy-tale setting: the lilting strains of a flute in the courtyard at dusk.

Engine Bowli, Falaknuma; 866/969-1825 or 91-40/ 6629-8585; tajhotels.com; doubles from $$$$.

The front parlor. Above: A marble fountain in the frescoed entryway.

SHAVIYANI ATOLL, MALDIVES

VICEROY

ON A FAR-FLUNG ARCHIPELAGO already known for fantasy getaways, the Viceroy Maldives finds new ways to raise the style stakes. The Los Angeles–based brand's first Asian property, located on a 17-acre private island in the country's undeveloped northern reaches, consists of 61 thatched villas whose shapes evoke the hulls of traditional Maldivian fishing boats. Interior design details, courtesy of Canadian firm Yabu Pushelberg, riff on the beachy setting, with nautical accents such as rope, raw wood, and canvas; glass-roofed rain showers embrace the pristine surroundings, while sunburst-patterned metal screens serve as a textural contrast to the white slipcovered sofas and drapes. At dusk, guests gather at Treehouse to lounge on cushions with their cocktails or ascend a swaying bridge for a prime seat over the lagoon. The scene is as glamorous as global travel gets.

888/622-4567 or 011-960/654-5000; viceroyhotelsandresorts.com; doubles from $$$$$.

188   A Beach Villa at Viceroy Maldives.

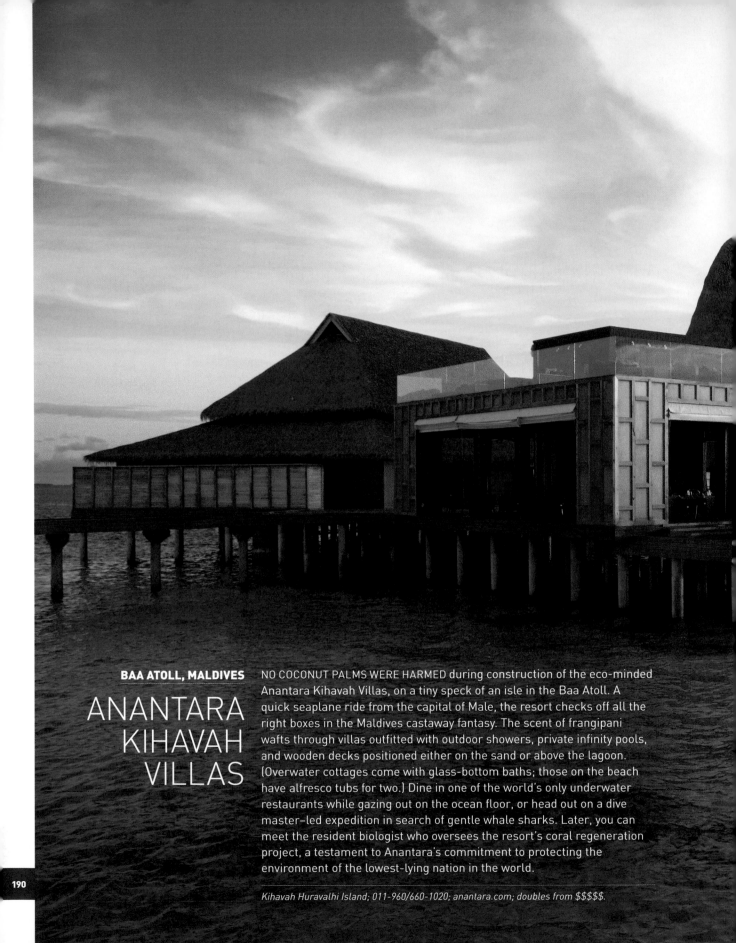

BAA ATOLL, MALDIVES

ANANTARA KIHAVAH VILLAS

NO COCONUT PALMS WERE HARMED during construction of the eco-minded Anantara Kihavah Villas, on a tiny speck of an isle in the Baa Atoll. A quick seaplane ride from the capital of Male, the resort checks off all the right boxes in the Maldives castaway fantasy. The scent of frangipani wafts through villas outfitted with outdoor showers, private infinity pools, and wooden decks positioned either on the sand or above the lagoon. (Overwater cottages come with glass-bottom baths; those on the beach have alfresco tubs for two.) Dine in one of the world's only underwater restaurants while gazing out on the ocean floor, or head out on a dive master–led expedition in search of gentle whale sharks. Later, you can meet the resident biologist who oversees the resort's coral regeneration project, a testament to Anantara's commitment to protecting the environment of the lowest-lying nation in the world.

Kihavah Huravalhi Island; 011-960/660-1020; anantara.com; doubles from $$$$$.

Sea.Fire.Salt.Sky.,
an over- and underwater
restaurant at
Anantara Kihavah Villas.

CON DAO, VIETNAM

SIX SENSES CON DAO

PHU QUOC MIGHT BE HAILED AS THE NEXT PHUKET, but those looking to go off the grid are venturing instead to the archipelago of Con Dao, an hour-long flight from Ho Chi Minh City. Until now, there was a dearth of decent places to stay on Con Son, the only inhabited member of the 16-island chain. But the arrival of the Six Senses Con Dao has been a game-changer, introducing a serious dose of luxury to the region. Along a pristine stretch of sand, the 50 minimalist villas have sloping roofs, canopy beds, and bathrooms with views of the South China Sea. In classic Six Senses style, the hotel's Vietnamese restaurant is set up to resemble a street market: separate stalls "hawk" noodles and rolls, while made-to-order dishes are cooked outside in charcoal-fueled woks. The authentically bustling atmosphere belies the slow, unhurried pace of your visit, from the first steaming bowl of *pho* at breakfast to a sunset dip in your private oceanfront pool.

Dat Doc Beach; 800/591-7480 or 84-64/383-1222; sixsenses.com; villas from $$$$.

Relaxing at Six Senses Con Dao, which overlooks the South China Sea.

Sofitel Phnom Penh Phokeethra's marble reception area.

SOFITEL PHNOM PENH PHOKEETHRA

THE OPENING OF THE SOFITEL PHNOM PENH PHOKEETHRA signaled a new era for a city once considered little more than a stopover on the way to ancient Angkor. The first international luxury hotel built in the Cambodian capital in more than a decade, the 201-room property blends contemporary style and colonial grandeur: marble-top sinks, delicate wooden ceiling fans, hardwood floors, and large windows that look out on the Mekong and Bassac rivers. The country's multicultural roots shine through in the hotel's restaurants. French cakes and pastries are served at the Chocolat bakery and café; Hong Kong and Cantonese specialties are on order at Fu Lu Zu; and Japanese *robatayaki* is the star at Hachi. In a destination now packed with stylish hot spots, from artisan shops to art galleries, the Sofitel serves up notice—Phnom Penh is back on the travel radar.

26 Old August Site, Sothearos Blvd., Sangkat Tonle Bassac; 800/763-4835 or 855-23/999-200; sofitel.com; doubles from $.

The Caroline Astor
Suite at the
St. Regis Bangkok.

BANGKOK

ST. REGIS

THE GLITTERING LIGHTS OF DOWNTOWN Bangkok surround you in this sophisticated cocoon of a hotel, the ultimate synthesis of business and leisure. Plush furnishings and Thai silk textiles add grandeur in each of the 227 rooms, while floor-to-ceiling windows summon the city's legendary 24-hour energy. But what really sets the property apart is its staff. Butlers are on call for tasks large and small (ask about the special St. Regis technique for packing a suitcase like a pro). Bartenders serve up the signature cocktail, a Siam Mary with just the right amount of bite, in a silver tankard. And at Southeast Asia's first Elemis Spa, therapists are trained in traditional Eastern modalities, which include an array of treatments designed especially for men. In a destination known for its sensory overload, the St. Regis represents a luxurious place to unplug.

159 Rajadamri Rd.; 877/787-3447 or 66-2/207-7777; stregis.com; doubles from $$.

asia

The Asadang's
front desk
and lobby lounge.

The Asadang Suite.
Right: Afternoon tea
served alongside
a neighboring canal.

THE ASADANG

WHEN IT OPENED IN 2009, the sepia-toned Bhuthorn hotel put owner-architects Direk and Chitlada Senghluang on Bangkok's design map. Now its sister property, the Asadang, is proving no less notable. It took the husband-and-wife team just seven months to convert the 19th-century mansion—located 900 feet from the Grand Palace—into an intimate bed-and-breakfast. The nine rooms, most named after local canals, serve as singular visions of Siamese heritage. Antique furnishings, traditional fabrics, and carefully sourced details (hand-sewn pillows; an artfully distressed mirror) cocoon guests from Bangkok's notorious hustle and bustle. For a getaway à deux, book the Rachabopit room, reached by a winding staircase and overlooking the temple complex next door.

94-94/1 Asadang Rd.; 66-2/622-2339; theasadang.com; doubles from $.

asia

A pool and walkway leading to Banyan Tree Samui's spa.

KOH SAMUI, THAILAND

BANYAN TREE

UNCHARTED BEACHES, RAMSHACKLE bungalows—that was then. This is Koh Samui now: high-style resorts and all the trappings of a newly anointed island of the moment. The Banyan Tree is one such asset. On a secluded southern-coast peninsula, its 88 villas are set along a steep, terraced hillside that tumbles down to a private cove. Buggies zip guests up and down vertiginous paths between the beach and the resort's three restaurants. Wake to a Gulf of Thailand dawn and walk 10 paces from your bed straight into your own generously sized infinity pool. Your butler—there's one for each room— can arrange for anything from a steaming cup of coffee to a diving excursion. And at the spa, your therapist will give you the best Thai massage you've ever had.

99-9 Moo 4, Maret; 800/591-0439 or 66-77/915-333; banyantree.com; doubles from $$$$$.

A sampling of tropical fruit. Above: The rattan headboard in one of the villas.

Raw bamboo
accents and alfresco
sofas at W Koh
Samui's Sip bar.

The private pool off of
an Ocean Front Haven villa.

KOH SAMUI, THAILAND

W RETREAT

BRINGING A DOSE OF MOD DESIGN to Koh Samui, W Hotels' first Retreat property in Southeast Asia hews to the brand's urbane aesthetic. The 73 glass-walled villas come with freestanding tubs and outdoor showers as well as private plunge pools and fire-engine-red espresso makers. The bright, youthful vibe extends to the public areas, where funky amoeba chairs and an oversize Connect Four game play right into the W target demo. Diversions that range from morning Thai-boxing classes overlooking the gulf to midnight mojitos at Woobar take advantage of the unimpeachable setting: a breezy plot on an arrow-shaped headland with beaches on both sides, one facing sunrise and the other sunset.

4/1 Moo 1 Tambol Maenam; 877/946-8357 or 66-77/915-999; whotels.com; doubles from $$$.

A Deluxe room at
Dune Hua Hin,
with a hanging lounger
on the terrace.

A shell curtain inside the Dune Deluxe room. Right: A suite's private pool.

HUA HIN, THAILAND

DUNE HUA HIN

YOUR FIRST IMPRESSION OF DUNE HUA HIN—Gulf of Thailand vistas notwithstanding—might be that of a boutique hotel anywhere in the world. The intimate beach retreat has just five minimalist rooms that are handsome yet familiar: designer furnishings; stone-walled bathrooms; freestanding tubs. But a closer look reveals immersive activities at every turn. Learn to make *tom yum* soup and *pad kee mao* (drunken noodles) during a private Thai cooking class in the hotel's wood-paneled restaurant. At your request, the chefs will prepare daily offerings of food, flowers, and incense for you to deliver to the neighboring monks, who will return the favor with blessings for a prosperous life. The hotel can also arrange for guides to take you to spot langurs and macaques at the Khao Sam Roi Yot nature reserve, an hour away. Anywhere in the world? There are few places you'd rather be.

5/5 Naebkhehars Rd.; 66-32/515-051; dunehuahin.com; doubles from $.

**A bedroom in one
of the shop-house
residences at
Straits Collection.**

PENANG, MALAYSIA

STRAITS COLLECTION

ERA-APPROPRIATE AMBIENCE ENVELOPS YOU at this jewel-box
hideaway that showcases Penang's bygone glamour. Owner
Narelle McMurtrie converted a row of Chinese shop-houses into
four residences that call to mind early-20th-century Asia:
latticed wood dividers; antique doors inset with colored glass.
Rooms are individually decorated, each with its own distinctive
character (don't miss one suite's alfresco wooden tub).
They're all within walking distance of China House, a compound
of shops, galleries, a performance space, and the Australian-
style Kopi C. Espresso Café. The sound of trishaws pedaling by
outside complements the scene.

89-95 Armenian St.; 60-4/263-7299; straitscollection.com.my; doubles from $.

A lounge off the lobby of the Fullerton Bay Hotel.

FULLERTON BAY HOTEL

THE MAMMOTH MARINA BAY SANDS casino complex may be Singapore's most-talked-about debut, but the real gem lies just across the water: the glass-and-steel Fullerton Bay Hotel, set near a 1930's pier that was the point of arrival for the island's first settlers. Today style seekers are beating a path to its door, drawn by the polished interiors from rising design star Andre Fu. Step through the monumental arch of one of the historic stone buildings and you're greeted by an enormous barrel-shaped chandelier over a marble mosaic floor. Upstairs, the 100 rooms are outfitted in rosewood, leather, and chrome, with terraces that maximize views of the skyline. Come nightfall, some of the best eye candy in town can be spotted at the slinky rooftop bar.

80 Collyer Quay; 65/6333-8388; fullertonbayhotel.com; doubles from $$.

asia

205

HOTEL VILA OMBAK

SEARCHING FOR THE BALI OF, SAY, 1970? You'll find it on Gili Trawangan, a tiny isle dotted with dozens of waterside cafés and reached via a 15-minute speedboat ride from Lombok. No motorized traffic is allowed here—guests arriving at the harbor take a horse-drawn cart to the island's southern coast, where Hotel Vila Ombak presides over a powder-white strip of sand. Thatched roofs, breezy Balinese-style *bale* pavilions, and outdoor showers in private gardens give the affordably priced property an authentic Indonesian air. The daily agenda is luxuriously indolent, involving nothing more than sunbathing or lounging by the tri-level saltwater pool with a *kelapa muda* (whole coconut). Craving an adrenaline rush instead? Fish for barracuda in nearby waters or hop the ferry to Mount Rinjani, an active volcano on Lombok where you can hike right up to the crater's rim.

Lombok; 62-370/614-2336; hotelombak.com; doubles from $.

A cluster of
Lumbung Seaside
rooms at
Hotel Vila Ombak.

GREATBARRIERREEFSYDNEYHUNTERVALLEYMELBOURNETAS
SYDNEYHUNTERVALLEYMELBOURNETASMANIAGREATBARRIER

AUSTRALIA +
NEW ZEALAND

The Walter Pavilion at the
Museum of Old & New Art,
in Tasmania, Australia.

HAYMAN ISLAND RESORT

IT'S CLEAR WHY HAYMAN ISLAND keeps topping those travel bucket lists. After five months of extensive renovations, the 726-acre, 210-room private-island getaway on the Great Barrier Reef has a sleeker, 21st-century look, from the dazzlingly white main building to the massive saltwater pool (roughly seven times Olympic size). Eight recently added glass-and-wood Beach villas, designed by Amanresorts architect Kerry Hill, are fitted with outdoor showers, private plunge pools, and Apple TV, and they open directly onto the sand with oversize sliding doors. A new botanical garden showcases more than 40,000 indigenous plants, with 40 different species brought in for fragrance alone. Man-made wonders aside, it's the reef that most come to see, and Hayman doesn't disappoint. At low tide, a sandy walkway emerges to lead guests right up to the edge of the coral—no boat required.

800/745-8883 or 61-7/4940-1838; hayman.com.au; doubles from $$$$.

One of eight
new Beach villas
at Hayman
Island Resort.

SYDNEY

SUNNY BEACH RESORT OR CULTURE CAPITAL?
Sydney is both—a destination that embodies
relaxed cosmopolitanism, from the
picture-perfect harbor district to the boho-
friendly streets of Darlinghurst. In three of the
city's top hotels, a sleek, sophisticated
vibe captures that inimitable Aussie energy.

1 PARK HYATT SYDNEY

Ideally positioned between
Harbour Bridge and
the iconic sails of the
Opera House in the
historic Rocks district, the
waterfront Park Hyatt
Sydney has reopened after
a buzzy yearlong, $65
million renovation. Among
the new additions are
three glass-walled rooftop
suites and 155 revamped
guest rooms courtesy
of Australian design firm
BarStudio. Sprinkled
throughout the public
spaces are original works
by homegrown artists,
as well as prints by
renowned photographer
Robert Billington.
ROOM TO BOOK Opera
King rooms feature
20th-century furniture
(think Eames recliners),
balconies made from
locally sourced timber, and
floor-to-ceiling views of
Jørn Utzon's masterpiece.
DON'T MISS Indulge in a
massage that incorporates
indigenous ingredients in
one of the spa's five
new treatment rooms.

7 Hickson Rd., The Rocks; 888/591-1234 or 61-2/9256-1234;
park.hyatt.com; doubles from $$$$.

An Opera View guest room at
the Park Hyatt Sydney.

▣ THE DARLING

Set among the rarefied shops (Chanel; Bottega Veneta) and restaurants of Pyrmont's multimillion-dollar Star complex, the 171-room Darling hotel offers low-key luxury at every turn. Pampering extras include a hammam and a spa pool scented with white tea and eucalyptus, a pillow menu and sumptuous goose-down comforters, and butler service.

ROOM TO BOOK Jewel suites have bespoke teak furniture, a wet bar, and a soaking tub.

DON'T MISS At Sokyo, on the hotel's ground floor, you can dine on former Nobu chef Chase Kojima's contemporary Japanese fare such as shishito peppers with shaved bonito flakes and Wagyu-beef short ribs. Or sample dishes by celebrity chefs, including David Chang, Teage Ezard, and Stefano Manfredi, at neighboring restaurants in the compound.

80 Pyrmont St.; 800/800-830; thedarling.com.au; doubles from $$.

▣ KIRKETON HOTEL

Retro glamour is the theme at the 40-room Kirketon Hotel, in edgy Darlinghurst. A glass-and-concrete façade gives way to marble floors and black-and-white photos in the lobby. Guest rooms have the minimalist air of a Manhattan loft, with mohair throws and wall-mounted flat-screen televisions; low-lit, French-inspired lamps add a touch of warmth.

ROOM TO BOOK Upgrade to an Executive room for 320 square feet of extra space, plus a king-size bed, a leather armchair, and a mosaic-tiled bathroom.

DON'T MISS Night owls gather at the Eau de Vie speakeasy, manned by the city's most talented barkeeps. On the imaginative menu: a flaming Ron Zacapa Blazer, a fiery cocktail made with rum, Pedro Ximénez sherry, muscovado sugar, and house-made bitters.

229 Darlinghurst Rd.; 61-2/9332-2011; kirketon.com.au; doubles from $.

The Darling's angular exterior.

Inside the Eau de Vie bar at the Kirketon Hotel.

Caves Beachside Hotel's
Bistro restaurant,
on Lake Macquarie.

HUNTER VALLEY, AUSTRALIA

CAVES BEACHSIDE HOTEL

TWO HOURS NORTHEAST OF SYDNEY, the Hunter Valley attracts two very different kinds of travelers: wine connoisseurs in search of the next great Chardonnay, and beachcombers looking for a quiet swath of sand. Both will find much to love about the Caves Beachside Hotel. The tented glass structure fronts Lake Macquarie, which is walking distance from the South Pacific shore, and has both a block of tidy white "motel rooms" for budget-conscious visitors and 18 suites with floor-to-ceiling windows, king-size beds, deep soaking tubs, and rain showers for travelers looking to splurge. Have breakfast on your private patio over the water before exploring the sea caverns at the southern end of the coast. Oh, and that next great Chardonnay? You might just find it an hour or so up the road.

7 Mawson Close, Caves Beach; 61-2/4980-9999; cavesbeachsidehotel.com.au; doubles from $$.

australia + new zealand

215

A street view of the sleek Crown Metropol. Below: Artwork in the hotel's lobby.

MELBOURNE

CROWN METROPOL

SUBTLE IT ISN'T, but what else would you expect from the continent's largest hotel? Welcome to the 658-room Crown Metropol, the S-shaped black-glass jewel in media mogul James Packer's Crown Entertainment complex. The sensory stimulation starts in the lobby with an oversize color-drip mural by Australian painter Noël Skrzypczak and spherical wooden sculptures by Korean artist Lee Jae Hyo. The on-site restaurants are just as compelling, featuring outposts of Donovan Cooke's and Neil Perry's respective culinary empires. Sybarites can book one of 12 soothing suites connected to the Isika Day Spa by private staircase, while high rollers can stake out a spot in the 24-hour casino. The final touch: a vertigo-inducing infinity pool on the 27th floor, where a swim proves as exhilarating as a win at the blackjack table.

8 Whiteman St., Southbank; 61-3/9292-6211; crownmetropol.com.au; doubles from $$.

Loungers and daybeds
lining the pool
on the 27th floor.

TASMANIA, AUSTRALIA

MONA
PAVILIONS

A CUTTING-EDGE CULTURAL institution might be the last thing you'd expect to find on a rugged Tasmanian riverbank. Yet multimillionaire David Walsh chose a cliff along the Derwent as the setting for his ambitious Museum of Old & New Art, the largest private museum in Australia. Steps away, the eight MONA Pavilions—with their bold geometric design, provocative artwork, and voyeur-friendly glass walls—are a fitting testament to Walsh's vision. Named after 20th-century artists and architects, the accommodations are as confidently curated as the museum itself, anticipating a visitor's every need: well-stocked kitchens; sinfully comfortable beds; a lap pool along the river; a destination-worthy restaurant. Add to this a winery and microbrewery and you'll see why the compound has been dubbed a Disneyland for grown-ups, where sophisticated meets subversive.

655 Main Rd., Berriedale; 61-3/6277-9900; mona.net.au; doubles from $$$.

Ocean vistas from
Oruawharo Beach House's
open-air courtyard.

ORUAWHARO BEACH HOUSE

AT 104 SQUARE MILES, "The Barrier" is the largest isle off New Zealand's North Island coast, but it's also the most untouched. Getting to Oruawharo Beach House may take some effort—following a 30-minute plane ride from Auckland, it's reachable only by four-wheel drive—but the sloping grasslands that surround it and the surreal blue expanse of the ocean just beyond are payoff enough. Sliding panels of floor-to-ceiling glass mean the line between indoors and out is virtually nonexistent. Designed by Kiwi architectural firm Fearon Hay, the minimalist timber-clad structure's four bedrooms are outfitted with low-slung furniture, fur throws, and jute rugs. (The house, which sleeps eight, must be rented one group at a time.) After you tramp through dense kauri woods or explore jagged inlets, the open-air courtyard provides the ideal setting for a no-fuss barbecue, with a sky full of constellations overhead.

S. Ringwood St., Torbay; 64-9/473-6031; ihu.co.nz; doubles from $$.

australia + new zealand

221

QUEENSTOWN, NEW ZEALAND

MATAKAURI LODGE

IT'S NO WONDER THAT HEDGE-FUNDER turned hotelier Julian Robertson chose this secluded South Island spot for his family's third property, Matakauri Lodge. Set on a lake backed by the snowcapped Remarkable Mountains, the lodge—sibling to the well-loved Lodge at Kauri Cliffs— is for travelers looking to ensconce themselves amid a pristine landscape without sacrificing their midday martinis. New Zealand designer Virginia Fisher kitted out the 11 suites with open fireplaces and simple schist-and-wood interiors accented in rust, orange, and cream. But most of your time will be spent outdoors: skydiving, jet boating, and killer downhill skiing are just an eight-minute drive away. Afterward, a massage that features heated basalt stones and essential oils keeps your adrenaline rush in check.

569 Glenorchy Rd.; 64-3/441-1008; matakauri.co.nz; doubles from $$.

Matakauri Lodge, overlooking
Lake Wakatipu and the
Remarkable Mountains.

WORLD'S BEST
AWARDS

NO2 HOTEL OVERALL
SINGITA SABI SAND AT SABI SAND PRIVATE GAME RESERVE
Kruger National Park, South Africa

TOP 100 HOTELS OVERALL

1 **SINGITA GRUMETI RESERVES (SASAKWA LODGE, SABORA TENTED CAMP, FARU FARU LODGE)** Serengeti National Park, Tanzania 98.44

2 **SINGITA SABI SAND AT SABI SAND PRIVATE GAME RESERVE (EBONY LODGE, BOULDERS LODGE, CASTLETON CAMP)** Kruger National Park, South Africa 97.95

3 **ROYAL MALEWANE** Kruger National Park, South Africa 97.88

4 **OL DONYO LODGE** Mbirikani Group Ranch, Kenya 97.71 ✪

5 **OBEROI UDAIVILAS** Udaipur, India 97.70

6 **TRIPLE CREEK RANCH** Darby, Montana 97.10

7 **MANDARIN ORIENTAL DHARA DHEVI** Chiang Mai, Thailand 97.00

8 **OBEROI RAJVILAS** Jaipur, India 96.92

9 **KIRAWIRA LUXURY TENTED CAMP** Serengeti National Park, Tanzania 96.71

10 **SERENGETI MIGRATION CAMP** Serengeti National Park, Tanzania 96.50

11 **LODGE AT KAURI CLIFFS** Matauri Bay, New Zealand 96.25

12 **FAIRMONT MOUNT KENYA SAFARI CLUB** Nanyuki, Kenya 95.64

13 **POSADA DE MIKE RAPU / EXPLORA RAPA NUI** Easter Island, Chile 95.47 ✪

14 **OBEROI AMARVILAS** Agra, India 95.33

15 **NISBET PLANTATION BEACH CLUB** Nevis 95.24

16 **LA RÉSIDENCE PHOU VAO** Luang Prabang, Laos 95.20

16 **FOUR SEASONS RESORT** Carmelo, Uruguay 95.20 $

18 **NGORONGORO CRATER LODGE** Tanzania 95.14

19 **PALACIO DUHAU – PARK HYATT** Buenos Aires 94.97

20 **MOMBO & LITTLE MOMBO CAMPS** Okavango Delta, Botswana 94.82

21 **HOTEL CARUSO** Ravello, Italy 94.75

22 **LITTLE PALM ISLAND RESORT & SPA** Little Torch Key, Florida 94.56

23 **MANDARIN ORIENTAL** Bangkok 94.49

24 **BLACKBERRY FARM** Walland, Tennessee 94.40

24 **STAFFORD LONDON BY KEMPINSKI** 94.40

26 **COUPLES TOWER ISLE** St. Mary, Jamaica 94.33

27 **STEIN ERIKSEN LODGE** Park City, Utah 94.32

28 **FOUR SEASONS RESORT HUALALAI** Hawaii, the Big Island 94.04

29 **RITZ-CARLTON BEIJING, FINANCIAL STREET** 94.00

30 **TURNBERRY RESORT, A LUXURY COLLECTION HOTEL** Ayrshire, Scotland 93.88

31 **OLISSIPPO LAPA PALACE** Lisbon 93.87

32 **SAN YSIDRO RANCH** Santa Barbara, California 93.86

33 **LE QUARTIER FRANÇAIS** Franschhoek, South Africa 93.82

34 **HOTEL VILLA CIPRIANI** Asolo, Italy 93.75

35 **HÔTEL PLAZA ATHÉNÉE** Paris 93.63

36 **FOUR SEASONS RESORT** Jackson Hole, Wyoming 93.60

37 **INTERCONTINENTAL BORA BORA RESORT & THALASSO SPA** French Polynesia 93.56

38 **SOFITEL LEGEND METROPOLE** Hanoi, Vietnam 93.51 $

39 **SINGITA KRUGER NATIONAL PARK (LEBOMBO LODGE, SWENI LODGE)** South Africa 93.50

40 **THE PENINSULA** Bangkok 93.49

41 **ELIOT HOTEL** Boston 93.47

41 **INKATERRA MACHU PICCHU PUEBLO HOTEL** Aguas Calientes, Peru 93.47

43 **TAJ LAKE PALACE** Udaipur, India 93.43

44 **THE PENINSULA** Chicago 93.42

45 **LONDOLOZI GAME RESERVE** Sabi Sands Wildtuin, South Africa 93.39

46 **HOTEL SPLENDIDO** Portofino, Italy 93.33

46 **MANDARIN ORIENTAL** Tokyo 93.33 ✪

48 **ONE&ONLY PALMILLA** Los Cabos, Mexico 93.22

49 **FOUR SEASONS RESORT** Chiang Mai, Thailand 93.14

49 **STEPHANIE INN** Cannon Beach, Oregon 93.14

51 **KATIKIES HOTEL** Santorini, Greece 93.07

52 **PARK HYATT** Milan, Italy 93.05

53 **BRENNERS PARK-HOTEL & SPA** Baden-Baden, Germany 93.00

54 **PALAZZO SASSO** Ravello, Italy 92.96

55 **DISCOVERY SHORES** Boracay, Philippines 92.93

$ DENOTES A GREAT VALUE (RATE OF $250 OR LESS)

✪ DENOTES A DEBUT ON THE WORLD'S BEST AWARDS LIST

Throughout the World's Best Awards, scores shown have been rounded to the nearest hundredth of a point; in the event of a true tie, properties share the same ranking.

NO5 SPA OVERALL
MII AMO, A DESTINATION SPA AT ENCHANTMENT
Sedona, Arizona

TOP 10 SPAS OVERALL

1 **RANCHO LA PUERTA FITNESS RESORT & SPA** Tecate, Mexico 94.79

2 **WESTGLOW RESORT & SPA** Blowing Rock, North Carolina 93.87

3 **CAL-A-VIE HEALTH SPA** Vista, California 91.91

4 **MIRAVAL RESORT & SPA** Tucson, Arizona 91.21

5 **MII AMO, A DESTINATION SPA AT ENCHANTMENT** Sedona, Arizona 90.82

6 **LODGE AT WOODLOCH** Hawley, Pennsylvania 90.19

7 **COPPERHOOD RETREAT & SPA** Shandaken, New York 89.33 ✪

8 **CANYON RANCH IN LENOX** Massachusetts 87.92

9 **CANYON RANCH HOTEL & SPA IN MIAMI BEACH** 87.51

10 **LAKE AUSTIN SPA RESORT** Texas 87.13

TOP 100 HOTELS (CONT.)

56 **COUPLES SWEPT AWAY** Negril, Jamaica 92.93

57 **FOUR SEASONS HOTEL GRESHAM PALACE** Budapest 92.90

58 **RESORT AT PELICAN HILL** Newport Coast, California 92.83

58 **RITZ-CARLTON NEW YORK, CENTRAL PARK** 92.83

60 **INN AT PALMETTO BLUFF, AN AUBERGE RESORT** Bluffton, South Carolina 92.80

61 **VILLA D'ESTE** Cernobbio, Italy 92.75

62 **OMNI BEDFORD SPRINGS RESORT** Bedford, Pennsylvania 92.71 ✪

63 **HALEKULANI** Oahu, Hawaii 92.69

64 **LE SIRENUSE** Positano, Italy 92.68

65 **CHANLER AT CLIFF WALK** Newport, Rhode Island 92.67 ✪

66 **ALVEAR PALACE HOTEL** Buenos Aires 92.58

67 **FAIRMONT MARA SAFARI CLUB** Masai Mara, Kenya 92.57

67 **HOTEL SAINT-BARTH ISLE DE FRANCE** St. Bart's 92.57

67 **HUKA LODGE** Taupo, New Zealand 92.57

70 **RITZ-CARLTON** Naples, Florida 92.56

71 **CROSBY STREET HOTEL** New York City 92.53 ✪

71 **ST. REGIS DEER VALLEY** Park City, Utah 92.53 ✪

73 **STOWE MOUNTAIN LODGE** Vermont 92.46 ✪

74 **KICHWA TEMBO TENTED CAMP** Masai Mara, Kenya 92.46

75 **TAJ MAHAL PALACE** Mumbai 92.42

76 **COUPLES SANS SOUCI** St. Mary, Jamaica 92.41

77 **WILLOWS LODGE** Woodinville, Washington 92.36

78 **MILESTONE HOTEL** London 92.35

79 **CAPE GRACE** Cape Town 92.35

80 **RAMBAGH PALACE** Jaipur, India 92.34

81 **THE LANGHAM** London 92.32

82 **CLOISTER AT SEA ISLAND** Georgia 92.32

83 **LADERA RESORT** St. Lucia 92.30

84 **AUBERGE DU SOLEIL** Rutherford, California 92.29

85 **HÔTEL DE PARIS MONTE-CARLO** Monaco 92.29

86 **ELYSIAN HOTEL** Chicago 92.25

87 **THE PENINSULA** Tokyo 92.24 ✪

87 **UMAID BHAWAN PALACE** Jodhpur, India 92.24

89 **RITZ-CARLTON, BACHELOR GULCH** Beaver Creek, Colorado 92.23

90 **INN AT SPANISH BAY** Pebble Beach, California 92.23

91 **ST. REGIS** Singapore 92.23 ✪

92 **ESPERANZA, AN AUBERGE RESORT** Los Cabos, Mexico 92.21

92 **PARK HOTEL KENMARE** County Kerry, Ireland 92.21

94 **VICTORIA HOUSE** Ambergris Cay, Belize 92.17 ⑤

95 **FOUR SEASONS RESORT MAUI AT WAILEA** Hawaii 92.15

96 **TRUMP INTERNATIONAL HOTEL & TOWER** Chicago 92.13

97 **SANCTUARY AT KIAWAH ISLAND GOLF RESORT** South Carolina 92.10

98 **FOUR SEASONS HOTEL GEORGE V** Paris 92.09

99 **EDEN ROCK-ST. BARTHS** St. Bart's 92.00

99 **EMIRATES PALACE** Abu Dhabi, United Arab Emirates 92.00 ✪

99 **FOUR SEASONS HOTEL MÉXICO, D.F.** Mexico City 92.00

99 **FOUR SEASONS HOTEL RITZ** Lisbon 92.00

99 **HYATT REGENCY COCONUT POINT RESORT & SPA** Bonita Springs, Florida 92.00 ⑤

99 **REGENT PALMS** Turks and Caicos 92.00

99 **ROSEWOOD MANSION ON TURTLE CREEK** Dallas 92.00

99 **SUNDANCE RESORT** Utah 92.00

NO1 CONTINENTAL U.S. + CANADA RESORT
BLACKBERRY FARM Walland, Tennessee

CONTINENTAL U.S. + CANADA

NO.3 CONTINENTAL U.S. + CANADA RESORT
SAN YSIDRO RANCH Santa Barbara, California

RESORTS (40 ROOMS OR MORE)

1 **BLACKBERRY FARM** Walland, Tennessee 94.40
2 **STEIN ERIKSEN LODGE** Park City, Utah 94.32
3 **SAN YSIDRO RANCH** Santa Barbara, California 93.86
4 **FOUR SEASONS RESORT** Jackson Hole, Wyoming 93.60
5 **STEPHANIE INN** Cannon Beach, Oregon 93.14
6 **RESORT AT PELICAN HILL** Newport Coast, California 92.83
7 **INN AT PALMETTO BLUFF, AN AUBERGE RESORT** Bluffton, South Carolina 92.80
8 **OMNI BEDFORD SPRINGS RESORT** Bedford, Pennsylvania 92.71 ⊙
9 **RITZ-CARLTON** Naples, Florida 92.56
10 **ST. REGIS DEER VALLEY** Park City, Utah 92.53 ⊙
11 **STOWE MOUNTAIN LODGE** Vermont 92.46 ⊙
12 **WILLOWS LODGE** Woodinville, Washington 92.36
13 **CLOISTER AT SEA ISLAND** Georgia 92.32
14 **AUBERGE DU SOLEIL** Rutherford, California 92.29
15 **INN AT SPANISH BAY** Pebble Beach, California 92.23
15 **RITZ-CARLTON, BACHELOR GULCH** Beaver Creek, Colorado 92.23
17 **SANCTUARY AT KIAWAH ISLAND GOLF RESORT** South Carolina 92.10
18 **HYATT REGENCY COCONUT POINT RESORT & SPA** Bonita Springs, Florida 92.00 ⑤
18 **SUNDANCE RESORT** Utah 92.00
20 **LITTLE NELL** Aspen, Colorado 91.85
21 **THE BROADMOOR** Colorado Springs 91.80
22 **FOUR SEASONS RESORT THE BILTMORE** Santa Barbara, California 91.79
23 **TIDES INN** Irvington, Virginia 91.73 ⑤
24 **WICKANINNISH INN** Tofino, British Columbia 91.67
25 **FOUR SEASONS RESORT** Whistler, British Columbia 91.47
26 **RITZ-CARLTON** Amelia Island, Florida 91.15
27 **LODGE AT PEBBLE BEACH** California 91.14
28 **INN ON BILTMORE ESTATE** Asheville, North Carolina 90.97
29 **VILLAGIO INN & SPA** Yountville, California 90.90
30 **THE GREENBRIER** White Sulphur Springs, West Virginia 90.64
31 **LAPLAYA BEACH & GOLF RESORT** Naples, Florida 90.44 ⊙
32 **SANDERLING RESORT & SPA** Duck, North Carolina 90.44 ⊙
33 **RITZ-CARLTON GOLF RESORT** Naples, Florida 90.40
33 **VENTANA INN & SPA** Big Sur, California 90.40
35 **SANCTUARY ON CAMELBACK MOUNTAIN** Paradise Valley, Arizona 90.27
36 **MEADOWOOD NAPA VALLEY** St. Helena, California 90.20
36 **MONTAGE** Laguna Beach, California 90.20
38 **TOPNOTCH RESORT & SPA** Stowe, Vermont 90.12
39 **FOUR SEASONS RESORT SCOTTSDALE AT TROON NORTH** Arizona 90.03
40 **FAIRMONT CHATEAU LAKE LOUISE** Alberta 89.95
41 **GRAND HOTEL** Mackinac Island, Michigan 89.85
42 **SURF & SAND RESORT** Laguna Beach, California 89.77 ⊙
43 **SAGAMORE RESORT** Adirondacks, New York 89.75 ⑤⊙
44 **ENCHANTMENT RESORT** Sedona, Arizona 89.73
45 **SOLAGE CALISTOGA** California 89.71
46 **TURNBERRY ISLE** (formerly Fairmont Turnberry Isle) Aventura, Florida 89.68 ⊙
47 **RITZ-CARLTON** Half Moon Bay, California 89.42
48 **ENCANTADO, AN AUBERGE RESORT** Santa Fe, New Mexico 89.33 ⊙
48 **ROYAL PALMS RESORT & SPA** Phoenix 89.33
50 **HOTEL HEALDSBURG** California 89.30

NO.1 CONTINENTAL U.S. + CANADA
LARGE CITY HOTEL
THE PENINSULA Chicago

CONTINENTAL U.S. + CANADA (CONT.)

LARGE CITY HOTELS (100 ROOMS OR MORE)

1 **THE PENINSULA** Chicago 93.42
2 **RITZ-CARLTON NEW YORK, CENTRAL PARK** 92.83
3 **ELYSIAN HOTEL** Chicago 92.25 ✪
4 **TRUMP INTERNATIONAL HOTEL & TOWER** Chicago 92.13
5 **ROSEWOOD MANSION ON TURTLE CREEK** Dallas 92.00
6 **WINDSOR COURT HOTEL** New Orleans 91.70
7 **BOSTON HARBOR HOTEL** 91.56 ✪
8 **SHUTTERS ON THE BEACH** Santa Monica, California 91.27
9 **SETAI SOUTH BEACH** Miami Beach 91.20
10 **FAIRMONT VANCOUVER AIRPORT** 91.11
10 **UMSTEAD HOTEL & SPA** Cary, North Carolina 91.11
12 **WALDORF ASTORIA** Orlando, Florida 91.03 ✪
13 **ROOSEVELT NEW ORLEANS, A WALDORF ASTORIA HOTEL** 90.96 $
14 **FOUR SEASONS HOTEL** Seattle 90.71
15 **HOTEL 1000** Seattle 90.67

16 **THE PENINSULA** New York City 90.63
17 **RITZ-CARLTON CHICAGO, A FOUR SEASONS HOTEL** 90.62
18 **FOUR SEASONS HOTEL** New York City 90.37
19 **FOUR SEASONS HOTEL** Boston 90.35
20 **WYNN** Las Vegas 90.12 $
21 **THE PALAZZO** Las Vegas 90.02 $
22 **MONTAGE** Beverly Hills, California 90.00 ✪
23 **ENCORE** Las Vegas 89.97
24 **THE PLAZA** New York City 89.96
25 **THE PENINSULA** Beverly Hills, California 89.96
26 **CHARLESTON PLACE HOTEL** South Carolina 89.87
27 **L'ERMITAGE** Beverly Hills, California 89.76
28 **HERMITAGE HOTEL** Nashville 89.70
29 **ST. REGIS** New York City 89.61
30 **HOTEL TEATRO** Denver 89.50
31 **RAPHAEL HOTEL** Kansas City, Missouri 89.38 $
32 **GRAND AMERICA HOTEL** Salt Lake City 89.33
32 **TRUMP SOHO** New York City 89.33 ✪
34 **ST. REGIS** Washington, D.C. 89.27
35 **HÔTEL PLAZA ATHÉNÉE** New York City 89.17
36 **FAIRMONT OLYMPIC HOTEL** Seattle 89.16
37 **MANDARIN ORIENTAL** Las Vegas 89.09
38 **MANDARIN ORIENTAL** New York City 89.06
38 **TAJ CAMPTON PLACE** San Francisco 89.06
40 **TRUMP INTERNATIONAL HOTEL & TOWER** New York City 89.04
41 **FOUR SEASONS HOTEL** Washington, D.C. 89.00
42 **THE CARLYLE, A ROSEWOOD HOTEL** New York City 88.90
43 **ST. REGIS** San Francisco 88.83
44 **ST. REGIS** Houston 88.80
45 **PARK HYATT** Chicago 88.70 ✪
46 **FOUR SEASONS HOTEL** Philadelphia 88.69
47 **HYATT AT THE BELLEVUE** Philadelphia 88.67 $
48 **THE HAY-ADAMS** Washington, D.C. 88.59
49 **LOEWS NEW ORLEANS HOTEL** 88.57 ✪
50 **TOWNSEND HOTEL** Birmingham, Michigan 88.57 $

SMALL CITY HOTELS (FEWER THAN 100 ROOMS)

1 **ELIOT HOTEL** Boston 93.47
2 **CROSBY STREET HOTEL** New York City 92.53 ✪
3 **XV BEACON** Boston 91.82
4 **MOKARA HOTEL & SPA** (formerly the Watermark Hotel & Spa) San Antonio, Texas 91.60
5 **RITTENHOUSE HOTEL** Philadelphia 91.50
6 **21C MUSEUM HOTEL** Louisville, Kentucky 89.43 $
7 **THE JEFFERSON** Washington, D.C. 89.29
8 **ROSEWOOD INN OF THE ANASAZI** Santa Fe, New Mexico 89.17
9 **ARIZONA INN** Tucson 89.04 $
10 **PLANTERS INN** Charleston, South Carolina 88.75 $

INNS (FEWER THAN 40 ROOMS)

1 **TRIPLE CREEK RANCH** Darby, Montana 97.10
2 **LITTLE PALM ISLAND RESORT & SPA** Little Torch Key, Florida 94.56
3 **CHANLER AT CLIFF WALK** Newport, Rhode Island 92.67 ✪
4 **LAKE PLACID LODGE** New York 91.56
5 **POST RANCH INN** Big Sur, California 90.99
6 **WHITE BARN INN & SPA** Kennebunk Beach, Maine 90.97
7 **THE WAUWINET** Nantucket, Massachusetts 90.67
8 **RABBIT HILL INN** Lower Waterford, Vermont 90.44 $
9 **MARQUESA HOTEL** Key West, Florida 89.90
10 **MAYFLOWER INN & SPA** Washington, Connecticut 89.88

CONTINENTAL U.S. + CANADA (CONT.)

HOTEL SPAS

1 **RITZ-CARLTON** New Orleans 98.00 ○
2 **OMNI BEDFORD SPRINGS RESORT** Bedford, Pennsylvania 96.50 ○
3 **FOUR SEASONS HOTEL** Las Vegas 95.00
4 **RITZ-CARLTON** Sarasota, Florida 95.00
5 **WICKANINNISH INN** Tofino, British Columbia 95.00

^{NO}**5** CONTINENTAL U.S. + CANADA HOTEL SPA
WICKANINNISH INN Tofino, British Columbia

HAWAII

RESORTS

1 **FOUR SEASONS RESORT HUALALAI** Hawaii, the Big Island 94.04
2 **HALEKULANI** Oahu 92.69
3 **FOUR SEASONS RESORT MAUI AT WAILEA** 92.15
4 **FOUR SEASONS RESORT LANAI, THE LODGE AT KOELE** 91.82
5 **TRAVAASA HANA** (formerly Hotel Hana-Maui & Honua Spa) Maui 91.53
6 **HAPUNA BEACH PRINCE HOTEL** Hawaii, the Big Island 89.75
7 **MAUNA KEA BEACH HOTEL** Hawaii, the Big Island 89.19
8 **RITZ-CARLTON KAPALUA** Maui 88.63
9 **ST. REGIS PRINCEVILLE RESORT** Kauai 88.47
10 **FAIRMONT KEA LANI** Maui 88.26
11 **MAUNA LANI BAY HOTEL & BUNGALOWS** Hawaii, the Big Island 88.22
12 **HYATT REGENCY MAUI RESORT & SPA** 88.20
13 **GRAND HYATT KAUAI RESORT & SPA** 87.96
14 **FOUR SEASONS RESORT LANAI AT MANELE BAY** 87.74
15 **FAIRMONT ORCHID** Hawaii, the Big Island 87.72
16 **ROYAL HAWAIIAN, A LUXURY COLLECTION RESORT** Oahu 87.39

17 **GRAND WAILEA** Maui 87.13
18 **KAHALA HOTEL & RESORT** Oahu 86.86
19 **WAILEA BEACH MARRIOTT RESORT & SPA** Maui 86.22
20 **SHERATON MAUI RESORT & SPA** 86.21
21 **JW MARRIOTT IHILANI RESORT & SPA** Oahu 86.00
22 **EMBASSY SUITES – WAIKIKI BEACH WALK** Oahu 85.29
23 **MOANA SURFRIDER, A WESTIN RESORT & SPA** Oahu 84.94
24 **KAUAI MARRIOTT RESORT ON KALAPAKI BEACH** (formerly the Kauai Marriott Resort & Beach Club) 84.54
25 **HYATT REGENCY WAIKIKI BEACH RESORT & SPA** Oahu 84.50 Ⓢ

HOTEL SPAS

1 **GRAND WAILEA** Maui 94.39
2 **FOUR SEASONS RESORT HUALALAI** Hawaii, the Big Island 93.23
3 **FOUR SEASONS RESORT MAUI AT WAILEA** 91.41
4 **RITZ-CARLTON KAPALUA** Maui 91.21
5 **GRAND HYATT KAUAI RESORT & SPA** 90.83

NO **1** HAWAII RESORT
FOUR SEASONS RESORT HUALALAI
Hawaii, the Big Island

NO 1 CARIBBEAN, BERMUDA +
THE BAHAMAS RESORT
NISBET PLANTATION BEACH CLUB Nevis

CARIBBEAN, BERMUDA + THE BAHAMAS

NO 1 CARIBBEAN, BERMUDA + THE BAHAMAS HOTEL SPA
COUPLES TOWER ISLE St. Mary, Jamaica

RESORTS

1 **NISBET PLANTATION BEACH CLUB** Nevis 95.24
2 **COUPLES TOWER ISLE** St. Mary, Jamaica 94.33
3 **COUPLES SWEPT AWAY** Negril, Jamaica 92.93
4 **HOTEL SAINT-BARTH ISLE DE FRANCE** St. Bart's 92.57
5 **COUPLES SANS SOUCI** St. Mary, Jamaica 92.41
6 **LADERA RESORT** St. Lucia 92.30
7 **EDEN ROCK-ST. BARTHS** St. Bart's 92.00
7 **REGENT PALMS** Turks and Caicos 92.00
9 **CURTAIN BLUFF RESORT** Antigua 91.29
10 **COUPLES NEGRIL** Jamaica 91.21
11 **JADE MOUNTAIN** St. Lucia 90.49
12 **JALOUSIE PLANTATION, SUGAR BEACH** St. Lucia 90.25 ✪
13 **MALLIOUHANA HOTEL & SPA** (currently closed) Anguilla 90.18
14 **RITZ-CARLTON** Grand Cayman, Cayman Islands 89.76
15 **ONE&ONLY OCEAN CLUB** Paradise Island, Bahamas 88.98
16 **SANDY LANE** Barbados 88.88
17 **CUISINART RESORT & SPA** Anguilla 88.29
18 **ANSE CHASTANET** St. Lucia 88.25
19 **ROCKHOUSE HOTEL** Negril, Jamaica 88.19 ⓢ
20 **JUMBY BAY, A ROSEWOOD RESORT** Antigua 88.17
21 **GRACE BAY CLUB** Turks and Caicos 88.08
22 **AMANYARA** Turks and Caicos 88.00 ✪
23 **THE REEFS** Bermuda 87.93
24 **RITZ-CARLTON** St. Thomas, U.S. Virgin Islands 87.90
25 **PARROT CAY** Turks and Caicos 87.85

HOTEL SPAS

1 **COUPLES TOWER ISLE** St. Mary, Jamaica 97.67
2 **COUPLES SANS SOUCI** St. Mary, Jamaica 95.87
3 **COUPLES SWEPT AWAY** Negril, Jamaica 94.11
4 **REGENT PALMS** Turks and Caicos 93.85
5 **SANDY LANE** Barbados 93.42 ✪

MEXICO

NO.2 MEXICO RESORT
ESPERANZA, AN AUBERGE RESORT Los Cabos

CENTRAL + SOUTH AMERICA

RESORTS

1 **POSADA DE MIKE RAPU / EXPLORA RAPA NUI** Easter Island, Chile 95.47 ★
2 **FOUR SEASONS RESORT** Carmelo, Uruguay 95.20 $
3 **INKATERRA MACHU PICCHU PUEBLO HOTEL** Aguas Calientes, Peru 93.47
4 **VICTORIA HOUSE** Ambergris Cay, Belize 92.17 $
5 **FOUR SEASONS RESORT COSTA RICA AT PENINSULA PAPAGAYO** 89.68
6 **LLAO LLAO HOTEL & RESORT, GOLF-SPA** San Carlos de Bariloche, Argentina 88.25
7 **JW MARRIOTT GUANACASTE RESORT & SPA** Costa Rica 88.17
8 **HOTEL ATITLÁN** Sololá, Guatemala 87.24 $ ★
9 **LOS SUEÑOS MARRIOTT OCEAN & GOLF RESORT** Playa Herradura, Costa Rica 86.19
10 **LODGE AT CHAA CREEK** San Ignacio, Belize 85.75

CITY HOTELS

1 **PALACIO DUHAU – PARK HYATT** Buenos Aires 94.97
2 **ALVEAR PALACE HOTEL** Buenos Aires 92.58
3 **HOTEL MONASTERIO** Cuzco, Peru 91.78
4 **PARK HYATT** Mendoza, Argentina 91.43
5 **FOUR SEASONS HOTEL** Buenos Aires 90.50
6 **HOTEL CASA SANTO DOMINGO** Antigua, Guatemala 90.36 $
7 **SOFITEL CARTAGENA** Santa Clara, Colombia 88.47 ★
8 **RITZ-CARLTON** Santiago, Chile 88.11
9 **JW MARRIOTT HOTEL** Lima, Peru 87.68
10 **GRAND HYATT** Santiago, Chile 87.27

HOTEL SPAS

1 **FOUR SEASONS HOTEL** Buenos Aires 94.58
2 **FOUR SEASONS RESORT COSTA RICA AT PENINSULA PAPAGAYO** 90.65
3 **LOS SUEÑOS MARRIOTT OCEAN & GOLF RESORT** Playa Herradura, Costa Rica 90.00 ★
4 **TABACÓN GRAND SPA THERMAL RESORT** Arenal, Costa Rica 86.49
5 **LODGE AT CHAA CREEK** San Ignacio, Belize 85.50 ★

NO 1 CENTRAL + SOUTH AMERICA RESORT
POSADA DE MIKE RAPU / EXPLORA RAPA NUI Easter Island, Chile

EUROPE

RESORTS (40 ROOMS OR MORE)
1 **HOTEL CARUSO** Ravello, Italy 94.75
2 **TURNBERRY RESORT, A LUXURY COLLECTION HOTEL** Ayrshire, Scotland 93.88
3 **HOTEL SPLENDIDO** Portofino, Italy 93.33
4 **PALAZZO SASSO** Ravello, Italy 92.96
5 **VILLA D'ESTE** Cernobbio, Italy 92.75
6 **LE SIRENUSE** Positano, Italy 92.68
7 **PARK HOTEL KENMARE** County Kerry, Ireland 92.21
8 **OLD COURSE HOTEL, GOLF RESORT & SPA** St. Andrews, Scotland 91.58
9 **GRAND HOTEL QUISISANA** Capri, Italy 90.86
10 **IL SAN PIETRO** Positano, Italy 90.58

LARGE CITY HOTELS (100 ROOMS OR MORE)
1 **STAFFORD LONDON BY KEMPINSKI** 94.40
2 **OLISSIPPO LAPA PALACE** Lisbon 93.87
3 **HÔTEL PLAZA ATHÉNÉE** Paris 93.63
4 **PARK HYATT** Milan, Italy 93.05
5 **BRENNERS PARK-HOTEL & SPA** Baden-Baden, Germany 93.00
6 **FOUR SEASONS HOTEL GRESHAM PALACE** Budapest 92.90
7 **THE LANGHAM** London 92.32
8 **HÔTEL DE PARIS MONTE-CARLO** Monaco 92.29
9 **FOUR SEASONS HOTEL GEORGE V** Paris 92.09
10 **FOUR SEASONS HOTEL RITZ** Lisbon 92.00

NO 2 EUROPE INN AND SMALL COUNTRY HOTEL
KATIKIES HOTEL Santorini, Greece

11 **HÔTEL DE CRILLON** Paris 91.91
12 **FOUR SEASONS HOTEL FIRENZE** Florence 91.51
13 **HOTEL IMPERIAL, A LUXURY COLLECTION HOTEL** Vienna 91.50
14 **RITZ PARIS** 91.15
15 **HOTEL DE RUSSIE** Rome 91.11

SMALL CITY HOTELS (FEWER THAN 100 ROOMS)
1 **MILESTONE HOTEL** London 92.35
2 **THE LANESBOROUGH** London 91.62
3 **MANDARIN ORIENTAL** Munich 91.50
4 **HÔTEL LE BRISTOL** Paris 91.00
5 **HOSPES LANCASTER** Paris 90.35
6 **THE GORING** London 90.18
7 **FOUR SEASONS HOTEL ISTANBUL AT SULTANAHMET** 90.00
8 **HOTEL CIPRIANI** Venice 89.88
9 **HOTEL D'ANGLETERRE** Copenhagen 89.87 ★
10 **HOTEL HASSLER ROMA** Rome 88.86

INNS AND SMALL COUNTRY HOTELS (FEWER THAN 40 ROOMS)
1 **HOTEL VILLA CIPRIANI** Asolo, Italy 93.75
2 **KATIKIES HOTEL** Santorini, Greece 93.07
3 **CHÂTEAU EZA** Èze Village, France 91.20
4 **DOMAINE DES HAUTS DE LOIRE** Onzain, France 91.05 $
5 **LES CRAYÈRES** Reims, France 88.73
6 **CHÂTEAU DE LA CHÈVRE D'OR** Èze Village, France 88.33
7 **LA COLOMBE D'OR** St.-Paul-de-Vence, France 87.73
8 **RELAIS IL FALCONIERE** Cortona, Italy 86.22
9 **LE PRIEURÉ** Villeneuve-lès-Avignon, France 86.13
10 **L'OUSTAU DE BAUMANIÈRE** Les-Baux-de-Provence, France 85.40

HOTEL SPAS
1 **ROME CAVALIERI, A WALDORF ASTORIA HOTEL** 96.92 ★
2 **FOUR SEASONS HOTEL GEORGE V** Paris 95.33
3 **FOUR SEASONS HOTEL GRESHAM PALACE** Budapest 92.73 ★
4 **FOUR SEASONS HOTEL FIRENZE** Florence 91.25 ★
5 **GRAND HOTEL QUISISANA** Capri, Italy 90.00 ★

AFRICA + THE MIDDLE EAST

LODGES AND RESORTS

1 **SINGITA GRUMETI RESERVES (SASAKWA LODGE, SABORA TENTED CAMP, FARU FARU LODGE)** Serengeti National Park, Tanzania 98.44

2 **SINGITA SABI SAND AT SABI SAND PRIVATE GAME RESERVE (EBONY LODGE, BOULDERS LODGE, CASTLETON CAMP)** Kruger National Park, South Africa 97.95

3 **ROYAL MALEWANE** Kruger National Park, South Africa 97.88

4 **OL DONYO LODGE** Mbirikani Group Ranch, Kenya 97.71 ✷

5 **KIRAWIRA LUXURY TENTED CAMP** Serengeti National Park, Tanzania 96.71

6 **SERENGETI MIGRATION CAMP** Serengeti National Park, Tanzania 96.50

7 **FAIRMONT MOUNT KENYA SAFARI CLUB** Nanyuki, Kenya 95.64

8 **NGORONGORO CRATER LODGE** Tanzania 95.14

9 **MOMBO & LITTLE MOMBO CAMPS** Okavango Delta, Botswana 94.82

10 **LE QUARTIER FRANÇAIS** Franschhoek, South Africa 93.82

11 **SINGITA KRUGER NATIONAL PARK (LEBOMBO LODGE, SWENI LODGE)** South Africa 93.50

12 **LONDOLOZI GAME RESERVE** Sabi Sands Wildtuin, South Africa 93.39

13 **FAIRMONT MARA SAFARI CLUB** Masai Mara, Kenya 92.57

14 **KICHWA TEMBO TENTED CAMP** Masai Mara, Kenya 92.46

15 **SABI SABI BUSH LODGE** Sabi Sand Reserve, South Africa 91.73

16 **EAGLE ISLAND CAMP** Okavango Delta, Botswana 91.40

17 **KEMPINSKI HOTEL ISHTAR** Dead Sea, Jordan 91.20 ✷

18 **GOVERNOR'S CAMP** Masai Mara, Kenya 90.75

19 **MALAMALA GAME RESERVE** Kruger National Park, South Africa 90.20

20 **SERENGETI SOPA LODGE** Serengeti National Park, Tanzania 90.10

CITY HOTELS

1 **CAPE GRACE** Cape Town 92.35

2 **EMIRATES PALACE** Abu Dhabi, United Arab Emirates 92.00 ✷

3 **FOUR SEASONS HOTEL CAIRO AT NILE PLAZA** 91.77

4 **FOUR SEASONS HOTEL CAIRO AT THE FIRST RESIDENCE** 91.74

5 **SAXON BOUTIQUE HOTEL, VILLAS & SPA** Johannesburg, South Africa 91.54

6 **MOUNT NELSON HOTEL** Cape Town 91.12

7 **FOUR SEASONS HOTEL** Amman, Jordan 90.00

8 **MENA HOUSE OBEROI** Cairo 89.48

9 **BURJ AL ARAB** Dubai, United Arab Emirates 88.97

10 **ONE&ONLY CAPE TOWN** 88.91 ✷

11 **KING DAVID HOTEL** Jerusalem 88.45

12 **TABLE BAY** Cape Town 88.00

12 **WESTCLIFF HOTEL** Johannesburg, South Africa 88.00

14 **GRAND HYATT** Dubai, United Arab Emirates 87.77

15 **FOUR SEASONS HOTEL ALEXANDRIA AT SAN STEFANO** Egypt 87.73

NO 4   AFRICA + THE MIDDLE EAST
LODGE AND RESORT
OL DONYO LODGE Mbirikani Group Ranch, Kenya

ASIA

RESORTS

1 **OBEROI UDAIVILAS** Udaipur, India 97.70
2 **MANDARIN ORIENTAL DHARA DHEVI** Chiang Mai, Thailand 97.00
3 **OBEROI RAJVILAS** Jaipur, India 96.92
4 **OBEROI AMARVILAS** Agra, India 95.33
5 **LA RÉSIDENCE PHOU VAO** Luang Prabang, Laos 95.20
6 **TAJ LAKE PALACE** Udaipur, India 93.43
7 **FOUR SEASONS RESORT** Chiang Mai, Thailand 93.14
8 **DISCOVERY SHORES** Boracay, Philippines 92.93
9 **RAMBAGH PALACE** Jaipur, India 92.34
10 **UMAID BHAWAN PALACE** Jodhpur, India 92.24
11 **DUSIT THANI LAGUNA** Phuket, Thailand 91.47 ✪
12 **UMA PARO** Bhutan 90.93 ✪
13 **PANGKOR LAUT RESORT** Pangkor Laut Island, Malaysia 90.00 ✪
14 **AMANDARI** Bali 89.87
15 **ANANTARA GOLDEN TRIANGLE RESORT & SPA** Chiang Rai, Thailand 89.71

CITY HOTELS

1 **MANDARIN ORIENTAL** Bangkok 94.49
2 **RITZ-CARLTON BEIJING, FINANCIAL STREET** 94.00
3 **SOFITEL LEGEND METROPOLE** Hanoi, Vietnam 93.51 ⑤
4 **THE PENINSULA** Bangkok 93.49
5 **MANDARIN ORIENTAL** Tokyo 93.33 ✪
6 **TAJ MAHAL PALACE** Mumbai 92.42
7 **THE PENINSULA** Tokyo 92.24 ✪
8 **ST. REGIS** Singapore 92.23 ✪
9 **THE IMPERIAL** New Delhi 91.77 ⑤
10 **PARK HYATT SAIGON** Ho Chi Minh City, Vietnam 91.74 ⑤
11 **MAKATI SHANGRI-LA** Manila 91.56
12 **TAJ MAHAL HOTEL** New Delhi 91.50
13 **MANDARIN ORIENTAL** Singapore 91.48
14 **THE OBEROI** Mumbai 91.27 ✪
15 **MANDARIN ORIENTAL** Hong Kong 91.02
16 **MANDARIN ORIENTAL** Kuala Lumpur, Malaysia 90.95
17 **THE PENINSULA** Manila 90.86
18 **RITZ-CARLTON** Kuala Lumpur, Malaysia 90.80
19 **SHANGRI-LA HOTEL** Bangkok 90.77
20 **THE PENINSULA** Hong Kong 90.70
21 **THE OBEROI** New Delhi 90.59
22 **ROYAL ORCHID SHERATON HOTEL & TOWERS** Bangkok 89.76 ⑤
23 **GRAND HYATT** Seoul 89.65 ✪ ⑤
24 **ISLAND SHANGRI-LA** Hong Kong 89.57
25 **FOUR SEASONS HOTEL** Singapore 89.50

NO2 ASIA HOTEL SPA
MANDARIN ORIENTAL Bangkok

HOTEL SPAS

1 **DISCOVERY SHORES** Boracay, Philippines 95.63 ✪
2 **MANDARIN ORIENTAL** Bangkok 95.35
3 **ST. REGIS** Singapore 95.23 ✪
4 **FOUR SEASONS RESORT** Chiang Mai, Thailand 95.19
5 **ANANTARA GOLDEN TRIANGLE RESORT & SPA** Chiang Rai, Thailand 95.00

NO 1 AUSTRALIA, NEW ZEALAND +
THE SOUTH PACIFIC LODGE AND RESORT
LODGE AT KAURI CLIFFS Matauri Bay, New Zealand

AUSTRALIA, NEW ZEALAND + THE SOUTH PACIFIC

LODGES AND RESORTS

1 **LODGE AT KAURI CLIFFS** Matauri Bay, New Zealand 96.25

2 **INTERCONTINENTAL BORA BORA RESORT & THALASSO SPA** French Polynesia 93.56

3 **HUKA LODGE** Taupo, New Zealand 92.57

4 **LILIANFELS BLUE MOUNTAINS RESORT & SPA** Australia 89.87

5 **REEF HOUSE RESORT & SPA** (formerly Sebel Reef House & Spa) Palm Cove, Australia 85.07

CITY HOTELS

1 **THE LANGHAM** Melbourne 90.55

2 **PARK HYATT** Melbourne 90.29

3 **INTERCONTINENTAL** Sydney 88.53

4 **PARK HYATT** Sydney 88.00

5 **SOFITEL QUEENSTOWN HOTEL & SPA** New Zealand 87.33

6 **FOUR SEASONS HOTEL** Sydney 86.87

7 **SYDNEY HARBOUR MARRIOTT HOTEL AT CIRCULAR QUAY** 86.84

8 **THE WESTIN** Sydney 86.18

9 **THE GEORGE** Christchurch, New Zealand 86.13

10 **THE WESTIN** Melbourne 85.65 ✪

Inside a Luxury
villa at the
Oberoi Rajvilas,
in Jaipur, India.

T+L 500

ALABAMA

BIRMINGHAM

⑤ Renaissance Birmingham Ross Bridge Golf Resort & Spa [88.00] Southwest of the city, a 259-room resort inspired by a Scottish castle, with a Robert Trent Jones golf course and the area's best spa. 4000 Grand Ave.; 800/593-6419; rossbridge resort.com; doubles from $–$$.

ARIZONA

PHOENIX/SCOTTSDALE

⑤ Four Seasons Resort Scottsdale at Troon North [90.03] Pueblo-inspired property (plus a renovated pool and a gastropub) surrounded by the foothills of the McDowell Mountains. 10600 E. Crescent Moon Dr., Scottsdale; 800/332-3442; fourseasons.com; doubles from $–$$$.

⑤ Hermosa Inn [88.47] An under-the-radar 34-room 1930's hacienda where highlights include Sunday barbecue dinners and an artists-in-residence program. 5532 N. Palo Cristi Rd., Paradise Valley; 800/241-1210; hermosainn.com; doubles from $–$$.

⑤ Montelucia Resort & Spa [87.90] Scottsdale's newest spa resort is a Moorish-inspired spread brimming with Spanish and Moroccan antiques. 4949 E. Lincoln Dr., Scottsdale; 888/627-3010; montelucia.com; doubles from $–$$.

⑤ The Phoenician, a Luxury Collection Resort [88.30] Newly upgraded resort on 250 acres with a $25 million art collection, three golf courses, and a Jean-Georges Vongerichten steak house. 6000 E. Camelback Rd., Scottsdale; 800/325-3589; thephoenician.com; doubles from $–$$$$.

⑤ Royal Palms Resort & Spa [89.33] 119 rooms, casitas, and villas (some individually designed) in a 1929 Spanish-inspired mansion on nine leafy acres near Camelback Mountain. 5200 E. Camelback Rd., Phoenix; 800/672-6011; royalpalmshotel.com; doubles from $–$$.

Sanctuary on Camelback Mountain Resort & Spa [90.27] Chic resort on the mountain; perks include a Watsu-pool-equipped spa and *Iron Chef America* winner Beau MacMillan in the kitchen at Elements restaurant. 5700 E. MacDonald Dr., Paradise Valley; 800/245-2051; sanctuaryon camelback.com; doubles from $$.

SEDONA

Enchantment Resort [89.73] 218 rooms and suites just off an $11 million refurbishment, plus the celebrated Mii amo Spa. 800/826-4180; enchantmentresort.com; doubles from $$.

L'Auberge de Sedona [87.65] Romantic creek-side retreat with a renovated spa that includes a massage cabana set among the trees. 800/272-6777; lauberge.com; doubles from $$–$$$$$.

TUCSON

⑤ Arizona Inn [89.04] Historic, 95-room pink-tinged adobe-style estate, piano bar, and pristine gardens. 2200 E. Elm St.; 800/933-1093; arizonainn.com; doubles from $–$$.

CALIFORNIA

BIG SUR

Post Ranch Inn [90.99] 41 solar-powered aeries made of wood, glass, and slate, cantilevered out from a cliff overlooking the ocean. 800/527-2200; postranchinn.com; doubles from $$$, including breakfast.

Ventana Inn & Spa [90.40] An adults-only hideaway: 57 rooms and 3 cedar villas, surrounded by 243 acres along the rugged coast. 800/628-6500; ventanainn.com; doubles from $$$–$$$$, including breakfast.

CARMEL

Bernardus Lodge [87.56] Provençal-inspired winery hotel, a celebrated restaurant, and an organic garden. 888/648-9463; bernardus.com; doubles from $$–$$$.

L'Auberge Carmel [89.00] 20-room inn that maintains a decidedly European feel, plus an exclusive restaurant, Aubergine (12 tables; 4,500 bottles of wine). 800/735-2478; laubergecarmel.com; doubles from $$, including breakfast.

HALF MOON BAY

Ritz-Carlton [89.42] Statuesque resort—261 rooms, 2 golf courses, a spa, and a vintner series—set on a cliff that fronts the Pacific. 800/241-3333; ritzcarlton.com; doubles from $$–$$$.

LOS ANGELES AREA

Beverly Hills Hotel & Bungalows [87.16] 210-room Dorchester Collection pink palace, now including 2 new Presidential Bungalows. 9641 Sunset Blvd., Beverly Hills; 800/650-1842; beverlyhillshotel.com; doubles from $$$–$$$$$.

Beverly Wilshire, a Four Seasons Hotel [88.27] Glamorous touches at this updated 1928 hotel include a Richard Meier–designed Cut steak house by Wolfgang Puck and a Rolls-Royce and driver for guest transportation. 9500 Wilshire Blvd., Beverly Hills; 800/332-3442; fourseasons.com; doubles from $$–$$$.

Four Seasons Hotel Los Angeles at Beverly Hills [87.79] 285 recently revamped rooms a mile from Rodeo Drive, with a 4th-floor pool scene. 300 S. Doheny Dr., Los Angeles; 800/332-3442; fourseasons.com; doubles from $$–$$$.

Hotel Bel-Air [91.71] 103-room Dorchester Collection sanctuary reenvisioned by a hotel dream team: Alexandra Champalimaud, David Rockwell, and Wolfgang Puck. 701 Stone Canyon Rd., Los Angeles; 800/650-1842; hotelbelair.com; doubles from $$$.

L'Ermitage Beverly Hills [89.76] Averaging 650 square feet, the rooms in this intimate hotel are some of the city's largest. 9291 Burton Way, Beverly Hills; 877/235-7582; lermitagebh.com; doubles from $$–$$$.

Montage Beverly Hills [90.00] Old Hollywood glamour in a new (2008) building on a prime L.A. corner. 225 N. Canon Dr., Beverly Hills; 888/860-0788; montagebeverlyhills.com; doubles from $$–$$$$.

Peninsula Beverly Hills [89.96] To celebrate its 20th birthday in 2011, this posh oasis added updated technology, including smart-phone check-in. 9882 S. Santa Monica Blvd., Beverly Hills; 866/382-8388; peninsula.com; doubles from $$–$$$.

Ritz-Carlton, Marina del Rey [87.20] Five miles from LAX, the 304-room hotel faces the harbor for expansive waterfront views and easy access to yachting. 4375 Admiralty Way, Marina del Rey; 800/241-3333; ritzcarlton.com; doubles from $$.

Shutters on the Beach [91.27] 198-room resort that exudes a polished coastal look (wicker furniture; subtle blue-and-white-patterned fabrics) and opens onto a beachfront bicycle path. 1 Pico Blvd., Santa Monica; 800/334-9000; shuttersonthebeach.com; doubles from $$–$$$.

NAPA/SONOMA

Auberge du Soleil [92.29] A favorite for nearly 30 years: the string of vine-covered *maisons* house 50 rooms; it also has 2 cottages. Rutherford; 800/348-5406; aubergedusoleil.com; doubles from $$$–$$$$$.

Calistoga Ranch, an Auberge Resort [88.73] 48 cedar-shingle lodges with open-air showers and a farm-to-table restaurant. Calistoga; 800/942-4220; calistogaranch.com; doubles from $$$–$$$$.

Carneros Inn [87.71] Secluded country cottages (private patios; heated bathroom floors; soaking tubs) in the bucolic Carneros wine region. Napa; 888/400-9000; thecarnerosinn.com; doubles from $$–$$$.

Hotel Healdsburg [89.30] Charlie Palmer's minimalist haven in Healdsburg's town square, home to the chef's Dry Creek Kitchen and a 500-bottle wine room. Healdsburg; 800/889-7188; hotelhealdsburg.com; doubles from $$, including breakfast.

Meadowood Napa Valley [90.20] 250-acre estate with a country-club feel, plus a wine-education program and Restaurant at Meadowood, one of only 2 Michelin 3-starred restaurants in the western United States. St. Helena; 800/458-8080; meadowood.com; doubles from $$–$$$.

Solage Calistoga [89.71] Family-friendly, hip, and modern: clean-lined cottages with cruiser bikes and a spa that specializes in mud therapies. Calistoga; 866/942-7442; solage calistoga.com; doubles from $$–$$$.

A block of Canyon View rooms at the Hotel Bel-Air, in Los Angeles.

Ⓢ **Villagio Inn & Spa** (90.90) A cozy, 112-room escape close to French Laundry that offers digital wine guides and unlimited champagne at breakfast. Yountville; 800/351-1133; villagio.com; doubles from $$, including breakfast.

ORANGE COUNTY

Ⓢ **Hyatt Regency Huntington Beach Resort & Spa** (87.56) Expansive Mediterranean-style resort with waterslides, surf instructors, and all 517 rooms redone in 2011. Huntington Beach; 800/233-1234; hyatt.com; doubles from $-$$.

Montage Laguna Beach (90.20) Craftsman-style resort on 30 oceanfront acres; all 250 rooms have floor-to-ceiling windows. Laguna Beach; 866/271-6953; montagelaguna beach.com; doubles from $$-$$$$.

Resort at Pelican Hill (92.83) Built in 2008, this Palladian-style resort has huge rooms (starting at 847 square feet) and one of the largest circular pools in the world. Newport Beach; 800/820-6800; pelicanhill.com; doubles from $$-$$$.

Ritz-Carlton, Laguna Niguel (89.04) Relaxed resort with Jean-Michel Cousteau–approved marine programs, plus a new Pan-Latin restaurant, situated on a bluff above a legendary wave break. Dana Point; 800/241-3333; ritzcarlton.com; doubles from $$-$$$.

St. Regis Monarch Beach (87.80) Sleek, 400-room golf-and-spa resort; the art collection includes works by Picasso and Chihuly. Dana Point; 877/787-3447; stregis.com; doubles from $$-$$$$.

Surf & Sand Resort (89.77) Relaxed oceanfront property, glowing from a 2011 renovation. Fun activities include beach yoga and stand-up paddleboarding. Laguna Beach; 800/524-8621; surfandsandresort.com; doubles from $$-$$$.

PASADENA

Ⓢ **Langham Huntington** (87.40) Spectacular gardens, a spa, and the new Royce restaurant in a polished 1907 hotel a short drive from the San Gabriel Mountains. 1401 S. Oak Knoll Ave.; 800/591-7481; langhamhotels.com; doubles from $-$$$.

PEBBLE BEACH

Inn at Spanish Bay (92.23) 269 rooms and a bevy of patios and fire pits, set 1,000 feet from the ocean and overlooking the Links at Spanish Bay. 800/654-9300; pebblebeach.com; doubles from $$$.

Lodge at Pebble Beach (91.14) One of the area's first hotels, dating to 1919; traditional rooms are warmed by fireplaces and have views of the 18th green of the Pebble Beach Golf Links. 800/654-9300; pebblebeach.com; doubles from $$$.

SAN FRANCISCO

Four Seasons Hotel (87.88) Glassy tower in the artsy Yerba Buena district, where you can take in skyline views from some of the city's largest guest rooms. 757 Market St.; 800/332-3442; fourseasons.com; doubles from $$$.

Mandarin Oriental (87.60) Celebrating 25 years and set on the top 11 floors of San Francisco's third-tallest building. 222 Sansome St.; 800/526-6566; mandarinoriental.com; doubles from $$-$$$$.

St. Regis (88.83) Contemporary interior spaces, plus an indoor pool, in a high-rise adjacent to the San Francisco Museum of Modern Art. 125 3rd St.; 877/787-3447; stregis.com; doubles from $$-$$$.

Taj Campton Place (89.06) Streamlined rooms, Frette linens, and a Michelin-starred restaurant, 1 block north of Union Square. Campton Place, 340 Stockton St.; 866/969-1825; tajhotels.com; doubles from $$-$$$.

SANTA BARBARA

Four Seasons Resort The Biltmore (91.79) Oceanfront grande dame frequented by celebrities. Tydes restaurant, at the beach club, recently launched an Italian-inspired menu. Montecito; 800/332-3442; four seasons.com; doubles from $$-$$$$.

San Ysidro Ranch (93.86) 41 private cottages and suites renovated to the tune of $100 million in 2009—set on 520 lavender-scented acres. Montecito; 800/368-6788; sanysidro ranch.com; doubles from $$$.

VENTURA

Ojai Valley Inn & Spa (87.79) Spanish-inspired spread that epitomizes indoor-outdoor living (alfresco fireplaces; nearby hiking trails), plus a 31,000-square-foot luxury spa and golf and tennis clinics for the whole family. Ojai; 888/697-8780; ojairesort.com; doubles from $$.

COLORADO

ASPEN

Little Nell (91.85) Tony ski-in, ski-out hotel with updated, Holly Hunt–designed interiors (stone gas fireplaces; sliding closet barn doors). 888/843-6355; thelittlenell.com; doubles from $$-$$$$$.

Ⓢ **St. Regis** (87.20) Handsome brick hotel fresh from a nearly $40 million renovation; ski butlers guide sporty types to the best powder. 877/787-3447; stregis.com; doubles from $-$$$$$.

BEAVER CREEK

Ⓢ **Ritz-Carlton, Bachelor Gulch** (92.23) Family-friendly gabled-roof lodge on Beaver Creek Mountain, with two resident canines and its own high-speed lift. 800/241-3333; ritzcarlton.com; doubles from $-$$$.

COLORADO SPRINGS

The Broadmoor (91.80) A 3,000-acre jumping-off point for horseback riding and fly-fishing at the gateway to the Rocky Mountains. The East Golf Course hosted last year's U.S. Women's Open. 866/837-9520; broadmoor.com; doubles from $$.

DENVER

Ⓢ **Hotel Monaco** (87.24) After a 2011 renovation, the 189 eclectic rooms at this business-oriented hotel—walking distance from the Colorado Convention Center—match the bold colors in the public spaces. 1717 Champa St.; 800/990-1303; monaco-denver.com; doubles from $-$$.

Ⓢ **Hotel Teatro** (89.50) Soaring ceilings and 600-thread-count sheets in a Renaissance Revival–style building across from the Denver Center for the Performing Arts. 1100 14th St.; 888/727-1200; hotelteatro.com; doubles from $-$$.

Ⓢ **Ritz-Carlton** (88.56) A glamorous 2008 addition; unexpected amenities include a rock-climbing wall in the 55,000-square-foot fitness facility. 1881 Curtis St.; 800/241-3333; ritz carlton.com; doubles from $-$$.

VAIL

Ⓢ **Sonnenalp Resort** (87.74) 115 suites and 12 standard rooms in a Bavarian-style lodge, the first hotel in the western U.S. to receive Sustainable Travel International LECS certification. 800/654-8312; sonnenalp.com; doubles from $-$$$.

CONNECTICUT

WASHINGTON

Mayflower Inn & Spa (89.88)
30-room English-country-style inn with a destination spa, surrounded by 58 garden-filled acres in the Litchfield Hills. 860/868-9466; mayflowerinn.com; doubles from $$$–$$$$$.

DISTRICT OF COLUMBIA

WASHINGTON, D.C.

Four Seasons Hotel (89.00) Brick hotel among 19th-century row houses; the spa features an indoor saltwater pool. 2800 Pennsylvania Ave. NW; 800/332-3442; fourseasons.com; doubles from $$–$$$$.

The Hay-Adams (88.59) Old-world elegance in an Italian Renaissance–style hotel across from the White House. 800 16th St. NW; 800/853-6807; hayadams.com; doubles from $$–$$$$$.

The Jefferson (89.29) Beaux-Arts jewel filled with Thomas Jefferson artifacts and gleaming from a recent renovation. A pianist plays Tuesday through Saturday nights at the wood-paneled bar, Quill. 1200 16th St. NW; 877/313-9749; jeffersondc.com; doubles from $$–$$$.

Ritz-Carlton Georgetown (87.90) Business-class digs in a brick-walled National Historic Landmark. 3100 South St. NW; 800/241-3333; ritzcarlton.com; doubles from $$–$$$$.

⑤ Sofitel Washington D.C. Lafayette Square (88.00) Art Deco–style hotel updated by Pierre-Yves Rochon, but retaining some original details (black marble floors; gold-leaf accents). 806 15th St. NW; 800/763-4835; sofitel.com; doubles from $–$$.

St. Regis (89.27) Two blocks from the White House, this 1926 Italianate hotel exudes historic elegance without feeling old-guard (case in point: the Rockwell Group–designed Alain Ducasse restaurant). 923 16th and K Sts. NW; 877/787-3447; stregis.com; doubles from $$–$$$$.

FLORIDA

AMELIA ISLAND

⑤ Ritz-Carlton (91.15) 444 rooms with balconies, and a roster of activities—

guided walks along sand dunes, kayak trips, and a new locally inspired Sunday brunch. 800/241-3333; ritzcarlton.com; doubles from $–$$.

CLEARWATER BEACH

⑤ Sandpearl Resort (88.92) LEED Silver–certified property in the central Gulf Coast, with an artists-in-residence program and boat slips located right across the street. 877/726-3111; sandpearl.com; doubles from $–$$.

FLORIDA KEYS

Little Palm Island Resort & Spa (94.56) Florida's most secluded and romantic retreat: a West Indies–style idyll set along a white-sand beach on a 6-acre island accessible only by boat or seaplane, which will also take you to a smaller island for a picnic. Little Torch Key; 800/343-8567; littlepalmisland.com; suites from $$$$–$$$$$.

⑤ Marquesa Hotel (89.90) 1884 clapboard houses and one of the island's best restaurants, set back from busy Duval Street. Poolside cocktail service is a welcome upgrade. Key West; 800/869-4631; marquesa.com; doubles from $–$$$.

⑤ Ocean Key Resort & Spa (87.23) Five-story resort (plus new 1-bedroom oceanfront suites) infused with Asian flair in the Balinese-inspired SpaTerre. The waterfront Hot Tin Roof restaurant serves caramelized grouper and crab-stuffed lobster. Key West; 800/328-9815; oceankey.com; doubles from $–$$$.

JACKSONVILLE

⑤ One Ocean Resort & Spa (87.25) 193-room resort (butler service; northeast Florida's only waterfront spa) on a 254-foot stretch of sand. Atlantic Beach; 800/874-6000; oneoceanresort.com; doubles from $.

MIAMI AREA

⑤ Biltmore Miami Coral Gables (88.00) Storied 1920's hotel and 3-year-old cooking academy surrounded by 150 manicured acres. Coral Gables; 800/727-1926; biltmorehotel.com; doubles from $–$$.

⑤ Mandarin Oriental (88.49) A 326-room tower on Brickell Key that includes an Asian spa and sushi restaurant. 500 Brickell Key Dr., Miami; 800/526-6566; mandarinoriental.com; doubles from $–$$.

A pool overlooking the Pacific at the Four Seasons Resort Lanai at Manele Bay, in Hawaii.

Ritz-Carlton Key Biscayne (88.00) 450 renovated rooms with a seaside theme, plus 4 restaurants and 11 tennis courts, on a barrier island south of Miami Beach. Key Biscayne; 800/241-3333; ritzcarlton.com; doubles from $$–$$$.

The Setai (91.20) A study in minimalism: 130 rooms and suites spread between a modern tower and a 1930's Art Deco building. Over-the-top packages include Ferrari rentals and helicopter tours. 2001 Collins Ave., Miami Beach; 888/625-7500; setai.com; doubles from $$$–$$$$$.

⑤ Turnberry Isle (formerly Fairmont Turnberry Isle) (89.68) This 407-room beach, golf, and tennis resort also features a skylight-topped spa and Bourbon Steak, by chef Michael Mina. Aventura; 888/721-3984; turnberryislemiami.com; doubles from $–$$$$.

NAPLES

⑤ Hyatt Regency Coconut Point Resort & Spa (92.00) 454-room family-friendly escape on 26 palm-shrouded acres along the Estero Bay. 800/233-1234; hyatt.com; doubles from $–$$$.

⑤ LaPlaya Beach & Golf Resort (90.44) 189-room seaside resort 15

minutes north of downtown, with a Bob Cupp–designed golf course. 800/237-6883; laplayaresort.com; doubles from $–$$.

Ritz-Carlton (92.56) A 450-room stalwart (plus 2 pools and a spa) set along the Gulf of Mexico's Paradise Coast. 800/241-3333; ritzcarlton.com; doubles from $$–$$$$$.

⑤ Ritz-Carlton Golf Resort (90.40) 295 rooms and 2 Greg Norman–designed courses that double as an Audubon sanctuary. A complimentary shuttle brings guests to the sister Ritz-Carlton hotel for access to white-sand beaches. 800/241-3333; ritzcarlton.com; doubles from $–$$.

ORLANDO AREA

Disney's Animal Kingdom Lodge (87.54) A 1,307-room lodge (and newly launched Spice Route–inspired Sanaa restaurant) a mile from the Animal Kingdom theme park. Lake Buena Vista; 407/934-7639; disneyworld.com; doubles from $$–$$$.

⑤ Hilton Orlando Bonnet Creek (87.58) 1,001 rooms and suites, plus a waterslide and lazy river, in a nature reserve set in Walt Disney World. Orlando; 800/445-8667; hilton.com; doubles from $–$$.

☉ Ritz-Carlton Orlando, Grande Lakes (87.88) 15-story tower modeled after an Italian palazzo, surrounded by 500 acres of lakes and trees, plus a Greg Norman–designed golf course. Orlando; 800/241-3333; ritzcarlton. com; doubles from $–$$.

☉ Waldorf Astoria (91.03) Three-year-old, 498-room hotel featuring elements of the brand's Manhattan flagship, including Sir Harry's Lounge. Orlando; 800/925-3673; waldorf astoria.com; doubles from $–$$.

PALM BEACH

☉ Brazilian Court Hotel & Beach Club (88.00) 1926 hotel with updated interiors, a Daniel Boulud restaurant, and a new beach club. 800/552-0335; thebraziliancourt.com; doubles from $–$$$.

The Breakers (88.70) A dramatic, palm-lined drive leads to this Italian Renaissance–inspired icon (5 pools; 9 restaurants; 11 tennis courts) on Palm Beach. 888/273-2537; thebreakers. com; doubles from $$–$$$.

Ritz-Carlton (87.57) Elegant yet relaxed resort along 7 acres of oceanfront property in the posh town of Manalapan; a $130 million makeover was completed 3 years ago. 800/241-3333; ritzcarlton.com; doubles from $$.

GEORGIA

ATLANTA

☉ Ritz-Carlton, Buckhead (87.48) 510-room high-rise well suited for workout buffs (there's a state-of-the-art fitness center and junior Olympic-size swimming pool), across from high-end shopping. 3434 Peachtree Rd. N.E.; 800/241-3333; ritzcarlton. com; doubles from $–$$.

GREENSBORO

☉ Ritz-Carlton Lodge, Reynolds Plantation (89.14) Lakefront resort just 75 miles from Atlanta, lauded for 99 holes of championship golf. Linger Longer Steakhouse, which closed after a 2009 fire, reopened last year. 800/241-3333; ritzcarlton.com; doubles from $–$$.

SAVANNAH

☉ Mansion on Forsyth Park (88.37) Over-the-top 125-room hotel (grand

piano; cheetah-print chairs) in an exquisitely restored 1888 mansion that also houses a cooking school and art gallery. 700 Drayton St.; 888/213-3671; mansiononforsythpark.com; doubles from $–$$.

SEA ISLAND

The Cloister (92.32) A 1928 Mediterranean-style mansion set on 5 miles of secluded beach. The hotel's new food truck serves Jamaican jerk chicken to go. 888/732-4752; seaisland.com; doubles from $$–$$$.

HAWAII

BIG ISLAND

☉ Fairmont Orchid (87.72) A recently refreshed 540-room hotel with lanais and hidden dining spots on 32 acres on the Kohala Coast. 800/444-4141; fairmont.com; doubles from $–$$.

Four Seasons Resort Hualalai (94.04) String of 2-story bungalows built upon ancient lava rock. Its updated Hualalai Spa now has 10 outdoor treatment rooms. 800/332-3442; fourseasons.com; doubles from $$$–$$$$$.

Hapuna Beach Prince Hotel (89.75) Secluded Kohala Coast resort complex on the Big Island's best beach, next to a state park lined with rocky outcrops. 866/774-6236; prince resortshawaii.com; doubles from $$.

Mauna Kea Beach Hotel (89.19) A $150 million renovation transformed this 1965 golf-and-tennis resort, originally built by RockResorts founder Laurance Rockefeller; on-site activities (hula classes; stand-up paddleboarding) make it a top choice for families. 866/977-4589; prince resortshawaii.com; doubles from $$$.

Mauna Lani Bay Hotel & Bungalows (88.22) Chic, eco-friendly 343-room resort offering updated tropical-style rooms and 2 golf courses on a 16th-century lava flow. 800/367-2323; maunalani.com; doubles from $$.

KAUAI

Grand Hyatt Kauai Resort & Spa (87.96) 602-room resort with 4 pools, a cliff-top Robert Trent Jones Jr.–designed golf course, and, as of last spring, bathrooms with rain showers. 800/233-1234; hyatt.com; doubles from $$–$$$.

St. Regis Princeville Resort (88.47) Terraced hotel (soaking tubs; infinity pools; a restaurant by Jean-Georges Vongerichten), on the island's north shore. 877/787-3447; stregis. com; doubles from $$–$$$$$.

LANAI

Four Seasons Resort Lanai at Manele Bay (87.74) 236-room beach resort geared toward urbanites who return for cliff-top golf and "snuba," a combination of snorkeling and scuba diving. 800/332-3442; fourseasons.com; doubles from $$.

Four Seasons Resort Lanai, The Lodge at Koele (91.82) Hawaii meets wood-sided country estate: Manele Bay's 20-acre sister property has a traditional English tea, nearby stables, and cultural programs. 800/332-3442; four seasons.com; doubles from $$.

MAUI

Fairmont Kea Lani (88.26) 450-suite escape on a calm cove ideal for whale-watching. Ko, a renovated farm-to-table restaurant, opened in April 2012. 800/441-1414; fairmont.com; doubles from $$–$$$.

Four Seasons Resort Maui at Wailea (92.15) A favorite celebrity hideout: 380 rooms and a slew of activities (outrigger canoeing; expert-led surf and cycling programs). 800/332-3442; four seasons.com; doubles from $$–$$$.

☉ Hyatt Regency Maui Resort & Spa (88.20) Mega-resort in Lahaina on the Kaanapali Coast with Hawaiian and Polynesian artwork and an outdoor theater for Cirque du Soleil performances. 800/233-1234; hyatt.com; doubles from $–$$.

Ritz-Carlton Kapalua (88.63) Former pineapple plantation known for its eco programs. An adults-only pool opened in 2010. 800/241-3333; ritzcarlton.com; doubles from $$$.

Travaasa Hana (formerly Hotel Hána-Maui & Honua Spa) (91.53) A quiet alternative to Maui's mega-resorts, now overseen by Denver-based owners. The 47 cottages and 23 suites are set on a seaside bluff. 855/868-7282; travaasa.com; doubles from $$.

OAHU

Halekulani (92.69) This century-old, 5-acre gem on Waikiki Beach—with 3 open-air restaurants, 3 Premier suites (including one by Vera Wang), and views of Diamond Head—will remain open through a renovation expected to be completed in June 2012. 800/367-2343; halekulani.com; doubles from $$.

Royal Hawaiian, a Luxury Collection Resort (87.39) Landmark flamingo-pink property where most rooms have views of Diamond Head. The Royal Beach Tower glitters after a $10 million renovation last year. 800/325-3589; royal-hawaiian.com; doubles from $$–$$$.

ILLINOIS

CHICAGO

☉ Conrad Chicago (87.69) 311-room business hotel and Lowcountry-inspired Terrace Rooftop (po'boy sliders; skillet cornbread) near Rush Street's popular dining spots. 521 N. Rush St.; 800/266-7237; conradhotels. com; doubles from $–$$.

The Elysian (92.25) A luxurious 2009 addition to the heart of Chicago's Gold Coast with a design aesthetic that recalls 1920's Paris, a Michelin 2-starred restaurant, and a no-tipping policy—an unexpected perk. 11 E. Walton; 800/500-8511; elysian hotels.com; doubles from $$–$$$.

Four Seasons Hotel (88.33) Floors 30 through 46 of a skyscraper overlooking Lake Michigan, upgraded after a $37 million renovation in 2010. 120 E. Delaware Place; 800/332-3442; fourseasons. com; doubles from $$–$$$.

Park Hyatt (88.70) 198-room hotel on Water Tower Square. New soaking tubs are situated for views of the lake and the Museum of Contemporary Art. 800 N. Michigan Ave.; 877/875-4658; park.hyatt.com; doubles from $$–$$$.

Peninsula Chicago (93.42) Sleek, 20-story state-of-the-art hotel with 3 restaurants, including Shanghai Terrace and the Lobby—and a 15,000-square-foot Espa in the heart of the Magnificent Mile shopping district. 108 E. Superior St.; 866/382-8388; peninsula.com; doubles from $$–$$$.

Ritz-Carlton, a Four Seasons Hotel (90.62) Across the street from the Hancock Observatory, with a lavish lobby (marble fountain; Art Nouveau–style reliefs) and 435 renovated rooms. 160 E. Pearson St.; 800/332-3442; fourseasons.com; doubles from $$.

Trump International Hotel & Tower (92.13) 339 rooms, a 23,000-square-foot spa, and Michelin-starred restaurant, Sixteen—all in a 92-story stainless-steel monolith next to the Chicago River. 401 N. Wabash Ave.; 855/878-6700; trumpchicago hotel.com; doubles from $$$.

KENTUCKY

LOUISVILLE

⑤ **Brown Hotel** (88.56) 16-story 1923 hotel with ornate old-world architecture and Kentucky Derby touches (equestrian art; horse-patterned throws). 335 W. Broadway; 888/888-5252; brownhotel.com; doubles from $–$$.

⑤ **21c Museum Hotel** (89.43) A trendsetting spot: 90 spare-but-polished rooms and a collection of works by living artists, all set in a complex of 19th-century warehouses. 700 W. Main St.; 877/217-6400; 21cmuseumhotel. com; doubles from $–$$.

LOUISIANA

NEW ORLEANS

⑤ **Loews New Orleans Hotel** (88.57) A 21-story, 21st-century glass box, plus a Creole bistro, located between the French Quarter and the Arts District. 300 Poydras St.; 800/235-6397; loewshotels.com; doubles from $–$$.

⑤ **Ritz-Carlton** (88.08) Converted department store a block from Bourbon Street. Post-Katrina, the hotel underwent a $150 million renovation, and the Francophile interiors were recently refreshed. 921 Canal St.; 800/241-3333; ritzcarlton. com; doubles from $–$$.

⑤ **Roosevelt Hotel New Orleans, a Waldorf Astoria Hotel** (90.96) Grand 19th-century hotel adjacent to the French Quarter, featuring the iconic Sazerac Bar and Domenica, by *Next Iron Chef*'s John Besh. 123 Baronne St.;

800/925-3673; waldorfastoria.com; doubles from $–$$.

⑤ **Windsor Court Hotel** (91.70) 316 traditional rooms—mainly suites spruced up after a $22 million 2011 restoration—in the Central Business District. 300 Gravier St.; 888/596-0955; windsorcourthotel.com; doubles from $–$$.

MAINE

KENNEBUNKPORT

White Barn Inn & Spa (90.97) 19th-century buildings furnished with sleigh beds and rain showers. The acclaimed namesake restaurant changes its prix fixe menu every week. 207/967-2321; whitebarninn.com; doubles from $$, including breakfast.

MARYLAND

ST. MICHAELS

Inn at Perry Cabin (89.04) Colonial-style 1816 manor—a classic Eastern Shore inn—on a private Chesapeake Bay inlet. 866/278-9601; perrycabin.com; doubles from $$.

MASSACHUSETTS

BOSTON

Boston Harbor Hotel (91.56) This just-updated 230-room hotel is the center of revitalized Rowes Wharf. Its bar boasts the city's largest collection of Scotch whisky. Rowes Wharf; 800/752-7077; bhh.com; doubles from $$–$$$.

Eliot Hotel (93.47) Neo-Georgian gem in historic Back Bay that's been family-owned for 70 years. Bathrooms are being updated with Bardiglio Italian marble. 370 Commonwealth Ave.; 800/443-5468; eliothotel.com; doubles from $$–$$$.

Four Seasons Hotel (90.35) 273-room brick luxury landmark (now offering cooking classes), across the street from Boston's Public Garden. 200 Boylston St.; 800/332-3442; fourseasons.com; doubles from $$.

Mandarin Oriental (87.43) A glamorous 2008 East-meets-West addition to Back Bay. Unique touches include crystal steam rooms.

776 Boylston St.; 800/526-6566; mandarinoriental.com; doubles from $$–$$$.

XV Beacon (91.82) Modern, 62-room boutique hotel (often just called "Fifteen") set in a Beacon Hill Beaux-Arts building. 15 Beacon St.; 877/982-3226; xvbeacon.com; doubles from $$.

CAPE COD

⑤ **Wequassett Resort & Golf Club** (87.64) The Cape's largest resort, on Pleasant Bay. Harbor views are best from the chaise-dotted lawns, the patio, and the 40 Signature Collection rooms. Chatham; 800/225-7125; wequassett.com; doubles from $–$$$.

MARTHA'S VINEYARD

⑤ **Harbor View Hotel & Resort** (87.47) 1891 mansion and cottages overlooking Chappaquiddick Island, suffused with Yankee beach style (gingham prints; teak rockers). 800/225-6005; harbor-view.com; doubles from $–$$.

NANTUCKET

⑤ **The Wauwinet** (90.67) On a stretch of sand between Nantucket Sound and the Atlantic, catering to adults (no kids under 12) with wine tastings and a spa. 800/426-8718; wauwinet. com; doubles from $–$$$, including breakfast.

⑤ **White Elephant** (88.44) Nantucket Town's largest resort, on a prime spot on the harbor. The expansive patio is a trump card. 800/445-6574; whiteelephanthotel.com; doubles from $–$$$$.

MICHIGAN

BIRMINGHAM

Townsend Hotel (88.57) 150 rooms plus a traditional afternoon tea, in a gilded Detroit suburb. 800/548-4172; townsendhotel.com; doubles from $$.

MACKINAC ISLAND

Grand Hotel (89.85) Grand colonnaded retreat built in 1887, with a 660-foot porch facing the Straits of Mackinac. 800/334-7263; grandhotel.com; doubles from $$, including breakfast and dinner.

MISSOURI

KANSAS CITY

⑤ **Raphael Hotel** (89.38) A 1920's Renaissance Revival–style hotel with an opulent lobby, overlooking the Country Club Plaza shopping center. 325 Ward Pkwy.; 800/821-5343; raphaelkc.com; doubles from $.

MONTANA

DARBY

Triple Creek Ranch (97.10) Adults-only mountain retreat on thousands of acres, with plush log cabins (wood-burning fireplaces; hot tubs), a 2,000-plus-bottle wine cellar, and a rotating collection of original art. 800/654-2943; triplecreekranch.com; doubles from $$$$, including meals.

NEVADA

LAS VEGAS

⑤ **Bellagio** (88.92) A mid-Strip extravaganza: 14 restaurants, dancing fountains, and Hyde, a new lounge by Philippe Starck. 3600 Las Vegas Blvd. S.; 888/987-6667; bellagio.com; doubles from $–$$$$.

⑤ **Encore at Wynn** (89.97) Steve Wynn's second Vegas resort is less glam and more desert oasis; the Encore Beach Club has 3 tiered pools and 40-foot palm trees; the casino has windows for natural light. 3121 Las Vegas Blvd. S.; 888/320-7123; wynnlasvegas.com; doubles from $.

⑤ **Four Seasons Hotel** (87.75) One of the more tranquil Vegas hotels, thanks to a hushed marble entrance, no casino, and a set-off location on the southern end of the Strip. 3960 Las Vegas Blvd. S.; 800/332-3442; fourseasons.com; doubles from $–$$.

Mandarin Oriental (89.09) Asian-inspired interiors by Adam D. Tihany and the first U.S. restaurant by French chef Pierre Gagnaire in a non-gaming hotel in CityCenter. 3752 Las Vegas Blvd. S.; 800/526-6566; mandarin oriental.com; doubles from $$.

⑤ **The Palazzo** (90.02) All-suite property with a Canyon Ranch SpaClub, Barneys New York, and 4 lounges including a champagne bar. 3325 Las Vegas Blvd. S.; 866/263-

3001; palazzolasvegas.com; doubles from $–$$$.

🏨 **Trump International Hotel** (88.00) 1,282-suite golden tower next to Fashion Show Mall. Family-friendly perks include spacious units with kitchenettes, board games, and children's books. 2000 Fashion Show Dr.; 855/878-6700; trumphotelcollection.com; doubles from $.

🏨 **Venetian Resort Hotel** (87.31) Inspired by its namesake city (canals; gondolas; even a piazza), with some of the largest rooms on the Strip and a new sports lounge. 3355 Las Vegas Blvd. S.; 866/659-9643; venetian.com; doubles from $–$$$.

🏨 **Wynn** (90.12) The flagship property from developer Steve Wynn has 2,716 rooms, gardens, and 14 restaurants, including the new wine-focused La Cave. 3131 Las Vegas Blvd. S.; 888/320-7123; wynnlasvegas.com; doubles from $.

NEW MEXICO

SANTA FE

🏨 **Encantado, an Auberge Resort** (89.33) 57-acre spa resort and on-site art gallery, set against the Sangre de Cristo Mountains, 10 miles outside the city. 198 State Rd. 592; 877/262-4666; encantadoresort.com; doubles from $$–$$$.

🏨 **Rosewood Inn of the Anasazi** (89.17) 58-room boutique property with Native American style (wood-beamed ceilings; kiva fireplaces), steps from Santa Fe Plaza's museums. 113 Washington Ave.; 888/767-3966; rosewoodhotels.com; doubles from $.

NEW YORK

ADIRONDACKS

Lake Placid Lodge (91.56) 30 waterfront guest rooms, all done up

Breakfast on the patio at Wynn's Terrace Point Café, in Las Vegas.

in chic Adirondack Arts and Crafts style, and a new teaching kitchen for 4 different cooking classes. Lake Placid; 877/523-2700; lakeplacidlodge. com; doubles from $$$–$$$$, including breakfast.

🏨 **Sagamore Resort** (89.75) 381-room resort, fresh from a $20 million renovation that added a pool, on a private island in Lake George. Bolton Landing; 866/385-6221; thesagamore. com; doubles from $–$$.

Whiteface Lodge Resort & Spa (87.53) Rustic, all-suite lodge featuring Douglas fir beams and cast-iron fireplaces, plus a bowling alley, kayaks, and paddleboats. Lake Placid; 800/903-4045; thewhite facelodge.com; doubles from $$, including breakfast.

NEW YORK CITY

The Carlyle, A Rosewood Hotel (88.90) A 35-story Upper East Side icon close to Museum Mile with jazz performances at Bemelmans Bar and cabaret at Café Carlyle. 35 E. 76th St.; 888/767-3966; rosewoodhotels.com; doubles from $$$–$$$$$.

Crosby Street Hotel (92.53) Quirky, contemporary interiors by Kit Kemp at a LEED Gold–certified property on a cobblestoned block in SoHo. 79 Crosby St.; 800/553-6674; crosbystreethotel. com; doubles from $$$.

Four Seasons Hotel (90.37) Monumental marble and onyx lobby, L'Atelier de Joël Robuchon restaurant, and rooms that average 600 square feet, in an I. M. Pei–designed tower. 57 E. 57th St.; 800/332-3442; fourseasons.com; doubles from $$$$–$$$$$.

Hôtel Plaza Athénée (89.17) This 142-room retreat (now with a spa) set on a quiet, tree-lined street offers easy access to Madison Avenue's shopping scene. 37 E. 64th St.; 800/447-8800; plaza-athenee.com; doubles from $$$$.

Loews Regency Hotel (88.23) A legendary business hotel convenient to midtown and Central Park. A major renovation is scheduled for mid 2012. 540 Park Ave.; 800/233-2356; loews hotels.com; doubles from $$–$$$.

Mandarin Oriental (89.06) On the 35th through 54th floors of the Time Warner Center, with Asian-inspired details and a spa tea lounge. 80 Columbus Circle; 800/526-6566; mandarinoriental. com; doubles from $$$$.

Peninsula New York (90.63) Classic Beaux-Arts façade, modern interiors, chauffeur-driven Mini Coopers, and a new sun terrace for yoga classes, all near midtown shopping. 700 5th Ave.; 866/382-8388; peninsula.com; doubles from $$$$.

The Plaza (89.96) Landmark hotel at the corner of 5th Avenue and Central Park South with a food hall by Todd English and iPads in all 282 rooms for summoning your white-gloved butler. 5th Ave. at Central Park S.; 800/441-1414; fairmont.com; doubles from $$$$.

Ritz-Carlton New York, Central Park (92.83) 22-story limestone tower a block from 5th Avenue, with 83 Central Park–facing rooms that are furnished with telescopes (and bird-watching guidebooks). 50 Central Park S.; 800/241-3333; ritzcarlton.com; doubles from $$$–$$$$$.

St. Regis (89.61) Luxurious details (such as Waterford crystal chandeliers), Alain Ducasse's Adour restaurant, and the refreshed King Cole Bar, in a 1904 Beaux-Arts icon on 5th Avenue. 2 E. 55th St.; 877/787-3447; stregis.com; doubles from $$$$$.

Trump International Hotel & Tower (89.04) The Donald's glass property on Central Park recently underwent a $30 million renovation and has one of the city's top restaurants, Jean Georges. 1 Central Park W.; 855/878-6700; trumphotelcollection.com; doubles from $$$–$$$$$.

Trump SoHo (89.33) 46-story tower suited for stylish SoHo thanks to touches by Trump's daughter Ivanka: muted interiors and a traditional hammam. 246 Spring St.; 855/878-6700; trumphotelcollection.com; doubles from $$–$$$$.

NORTH CAROLINA

ASHEVILLE

🏨 **Inn on Biltmore Estate** (90.97) A 210-room mansion set on George Vanderbilt's 8,000-acre Biltmore estate, surrounded by the Blue Ridge Mountains. 800/858-4130; biltmore. com; doubles from $–$$.

CARY

Umstead Hotel & Spa (91.11) Tranquil 150-room food-focused property on 12 acres, minutes from the airport and downtown Raleigh. 866/877-4141; theumstead.com; doubles from $$.

DUCK

⑤ **Sanderling Resort & Spa** (90.44) Cluster of cedar-shingled buildings along 13 Outer Banks acres, ideal for ocean views and easy access to hiking trails. 800/701-4111; thesanderling. com; doubles from $–$$.

OREGON

CANNON BEACH

Stephanie Inn (93.14) Overlooking Haystack Rock; the 41 rooms are equipped with fireplaces, private balconies, Tempur-Pedic beds, and Jacuzzis in the overhauled bathrooms. 800/633-3466; stephanieinn.com; doubles from $$, including breakfast.

PENNSYLVANIA

BEDFORD SPRINGS

⑤ **Omni Bedford Springs Resort** (92.71) 2,200-acre getaway (brick-and-white-column façade; 216 rooms; 2 pools), in a historic town centered around mineral springs that's convenient to Philadelphia and D.C. 2138 Business Rte. 220; 800/843-6664; omnihotels.com; doubles from $.

PHILADELPHIA

Four Seasons Hotel (88.69) Eight-story hotel on Logan Square—the city's cultural heart—plus a well-regarded spa. 1 Logan Square; 800/332-3442; fourseasons.com; doubles from $$.

Hyatt at the Bellevue (88.67) Set in a 1904 historic building, this 188-room property (including 16 revamped suites) is located in Philly's burgeoning downtown. 200 S. Broad St.; 800/233-1234; hyatt.com; doubles from $$.

Rittenhouse Hotel (91.50) Prestigious address on Rittenhouse Square with the city's largest guest rooms. Public spaces display paintings by Mary Cassatt. 210 W. Rittenhouse Square; 800/635-1042; rittenhousehotel.com; doubles from $$–$$$.

RHODE ISLAND

NEWPORT

Castle Hill Inn (87.36) 19th-century Victorian mansion and recently redone beach house on a peninsula where the Atlantic meets Narragansett Bay. 888/466-1355; castlehillinn.com; doubles from $$, including breakfast.

Chanler at Cliff Walk (92.67) A 20-room hotel with rooms in plush Continental styles ranging from French Provincial to Regency, just 1 mile outside Newport, overlooking the Atlantic. 866/793-5664; thechanler. com; doubles from $$–$$$$.

WATCH HILL

Ocean House (87.80) 1868 Victorian manor, primed from a $140 million renovation, on a private Atlantic Ocean beach. 888/552-2588; oceanhousri. com; doubles from $$–$$$.

SOUTH CAROLINA

BLUFFTON

Inn at Palmetto Bluff, an Auberge Resort (92.80) Plantation-style resort on coastal marshland: 50 cottage rooms and suites, a spa, and outdoor activities (fly-fishing; holiday festivals). 866/706-6565; palmettobluffresort. com; doubles from $$–$$$$.

CHARLESTON

⑤ **Charleston Place** (89.87) One of the city's largest hotels, with a 1-to-2 staff-to-guest ratio and a pool set under a retractable roof. 205 Meeting St.; 800/237-1236; orient-express. com; doubles from $–$$.

⑤ **Planters Inn** (88.75) 19th-century building and modern addition with a popular restaurant, Peninsula Grill. 112 N. Market St.; 800/845-7082; plantersinn.com; doubles from $$.

Wentworth Mansion (87.75) A 21-room 1886 former residence and a small spa in the historic district.149 Wentworth St.; 888/466-1886; wentworthmansion.com; doubles from $$, including breakfast.

KIAWAH ISLAND

Sanctuary at Kiawah Island Golf Resort (92.10) Stately 255-room hotel on the grounds of a top golf resort. 877/683-1234; kiawahresort. com; doubles from $$.

SUMMERVILLE

⑤ **Woodlands Inn** (89.60) A 1906 Neo-Georgian mansion with 19 recently renovated rooms; a bastion of Southern hospitality. 800/774-9999; woodlandsinn.com; doubles from $–$$.

TENNESSEE

NASHVILLE

Hermitage Hotel (89.70) The city's choicest digs—with a stained-glass ceiling and marble columns—favored by country music stars since 1910. 231 6th Ave. N.; 888/888-9414; thehermitagehotel.com; doubles from $$.

WALLAND

Blackberry Farm (94.40) The ne plus ultra of rural luxury, with renowned cuisine, set on a farm in the Great Smoky Mountains. 800/648-4252; blackberryfarm.com; doubles from $$$$–$$$$$, including meals.

TEXAS

AUSTIN

Four Seasons Hotel (87.59) 291-room Southwestern-style property, newly revamped fitness center, and Trio, one of the city's best restaurants. 98 San Jacinto Blvd.; 800/332-3442; fourseasons.com; doubles from $$–$$$.

DALLAS

Rosewood Crescent Hotel (88.18) Limestone landmark and an outpost of chef Nobu Matsuhisa's namesake restaurant, in Uptown near the new Winspear Opera House. 400 Crescent Court; 888/767-3966; rosewoodhotels. com; doubles from $$$.

Rosewood Mansion on Turtle Creek (92.00) This 143-room former cotton magnate's mansion was updated in honor of the hotel's 30th anniversary in 2010. 2821 Turtle Creek Blvd.; 888/767-3966; rosewoodhotels. com; doubles from $$.

HOUSTON

Hotel ZaZa (88.14) Splashy interiors (zebra-striped chairs; huge, low-hanging chandeliers) in a historic

An entrance to the Inn at Palmetto Bluff, an Auberge Resort, in Bluffton, South Carolina.

property in Houston's central museum district, plus a lively bar scene. 5701 Main St.; 888/880-3244; hotelzaza houston.com; doubles from $$.

⑤ Omni Houston Hotel (87.48) Downtown 387-room hotel that houses 2 Texas-size swimming pools and a 7,100-square-foot spa. 4 Riverway; 888/444-6664; omnihotels. com; doubles from $.

St. Regis (88.80) A 232-room hotel with upscale charms (an on-site harpist; orchid arrangements), on a wooded lot near the Galleria mall. 1919 Briar Oaks Lane; 877/787-3447; stregis.com; doubles from $$-$$$.

SAN ANTONIO

⑤ JW Marriott San Antonio Hill Country Resort & Spa (89.21) 1,002 rooms in rolling Texas Hill Country, 20 minutes from downtown. 23808 Resort Pkwy.; 800/228-9290; jwmarriott.com; doubles from $-$$.

Mokara Hotel & Spa (91.60) The first property from Omni Hotels' new luxury brand, a minute's stroll from the Alamo. 212 W. Crockett St.; 866/605-1212; mokarahotels.com; doubles from $$.

⑤ Omni La Mansion del Rio (87.35) 1854 Spanish-colonial school transformed into a 338-room hideaway on the River Walk. 112 College St.; 888/444-6664; omni hotels.com; doubles from $.

UTAH

PARK CITY

⑤ Stein Eriksen Lodge (94.32) Norwegian-style mid-mountain chalet at Deer Valley ski resort, committed to raising $100,000 for cancer research through philanthropic programs. 800/453-1302; steinlodge.com; doubles from $$-$$$$, including breakfast.

St. Regis Deer Valley (92.53) Ski-in, ski-out compound with a restaurant by Jean-Georges Vongerichten and the only funicular at a mountain resort in the United States. 877/787-3447; stregis.com; doubles from $$$-$$$$$.

SALT LAKE CITY

⑤ Grand America Hotel (89.33) An opulent 24-story structure with 775

guest rooms and handcrafted Richelieu furniture, plus a new patisserie. 555 S. Main St.; 800/621-4505; grandamerica.com; doubles from $-$$.

SUNDANCE

⑤ Sundance Resort (92.00) Robert Redford's rustic-luxe retreat on 5,000 acres 45 minutes from Park City. 800/892-1600; sundanceresort. com; doubles from $-$$.

VERMONT

LOWER WATERFORD

⑤ Rabbit Hill Inn (90.44) Romantic getaway (candlelit breakfast; canopy beds) at a restored residence and tavern, both about 200 years old. 800/762-8669; rabbithillinn.com; doubles from $, including breakfast and afternoon tea.

STOWE

⑤ Stowe Mountain Lodge (92.46) The largest luxury lodge in Stowe, with mountain access, a Mercedes fleet, and a new performing arts center. 888/478-6938; stowemountainlodge. com; doubles from $-$$.

⑤ Topnotch Resort & Spa (90.12) The first full-service resort at the base of Vermont's tallest peak. The mega-spa and tennis clinic are area standouts. 800/451-8686; topnotch resort.com; doubles from $-$$.

⑤ Trapp Family Lodge (88.80) Austrian-style chalet (now with an on-site brewery) from the family that inspired *The Sound of Music*. 800/826-7000; trappfamily. com; doubles from $-$$$.

VIRGINIA

HOT SPRINGS

⑤ The Homestead (87.91) 1766 grand National Historic Landmark (157 renovated rooms; archery; off-roading) on 3,000 Allegheny Mountain acres. 800/838-1766; thehomestead. com; doubles from $-$$.

IRVINGTON

⑤ Tides Inn (91.73) Chesapeake Bay resort offering a roster of outdoor activities, from kayaking to croquet. 800/843-3746; tidesinn.com; doubles from $-$$.

WASHINGTON

Inn at Little Washington (87.39) Antiques and floral fabrics in a country-house hotel. Chef-proprietor Patrick O'Connell's American cooking is a highlight. 540/675-3800; theinn atlittlewashington.com; doubles from $$-$$$, including breakfast.

WASHINGTON

SEATTLE

⑤ Fairmont Olympic Hotel (89.16) Landmark property exuding old-world glamour (witness the Biedermeier-inspired furniture). 411 University St.; 800/441-1414; fairmont.com; doubles from $-$$.

Four Seasons Hotel (90.71) Downtown hotel on floors 1–10 of a 21-story building, with original art and views of Puget Sound, just steps from the waterfront. 99 Union St.; 800/332-3442; fourseasons.com; doubles from $$.

⑤ Hotel 1000 (90.67) High-tech and eco-friendly property with 120 modern rooms, 4 blocks from Pike Place Market. 1000 1st Ave.; 877/315-1088; hotel1000seattle.com; doubles from $-$$.

WOODINVILLE

⑤ Willows Lodge (92.36) Rustic-chic interiors and the state's first electric-car charging station, on 5 bucolic acres 25 miles north of Seattle. 877/424-3930; willowslodge. com; doubles from $-$$.

WEST VIRGINIA

WHITE SULPHUR SPRINGS

⑤ The Greenbrier (90.64) Renovated 1913 resort in the Allegheny Mountains, renowned for its design by Dorothy Draper and her protégé, Carleton Varney. 800/453-4858; greenbrier.com; doubles from $-$$.

WYOMING

JACKSON HOLE

⑤ Four Seasons Resort (93.60) Ski-in, ski-out lodge with fireplaces in every room and a team of adventure concierges. 800/332-3442; fourseasons.com; doubles from $-$$$$.

⑤ Snake River Lodge & Spa (89.05) A 123-room Teton Village lodge by RockResorts, plus Wyoming's largest spa. 866/614-7625; rockresorts.com; doubles from $-$$.

⑤ Teton Mountain Lodge & Spa (87.37) Mountainside convenience at the base of Jackson Hole, just steps from the aerial tram. 800/631-6271; tetonlodge.com; doubles from $-$$.

CANADA

ALBERTA

LAKE LOUISE

Fairmont Chateau Lake Louise (89.95) Grand 1890 resort and just-expanded 3,000-square-foot spa flanked by the Rocky Mountains. 800/441-1414; fairmont.com; doubles from $$.

BRITISH COLUMBIA

TOFINO

Wickaninnish Inn (91.67) Nature- and food-focused cedar inn atop a rocky promontory, with eco-initiatives to protect the nearby Pacific Rim National Park. 800/333-4604; wickinn. com; doubles from $$.

VANCOUVER

Fairmont Vancouver Airport (91.11) Sleek and quiet (triple-paned glass) tower above the U.S. departures area of Vancouver International Airport, 30 minutes from downtown. 3111 Grant McConachie Way; 800/441-1414; fairmont.com; doubles from $$.

Four Seasons Hotel (87.20) Centrally located 28-story high-rise next to the tony Pacific Centre mall. 791 W. Georgia St.; 800/332-3442; four seasons.com; doubles from $$.

WHISTLER

⑤ Fairmont Chateau (87.18) Ski-in, ski-out resort in the upper village, with a Robert Trent Jones Jr.–designed golf course. 800/441-1414; fairmont.com; doubles from $-$$.

Four Seasons Resort (91.47) A 273-room forest lodge located just a short stroll from Whistler Village.

800/332-3442; fourseasons.com; doubles from $$.

QUEBEC

QUEBEC CITY

❺ **Auberge Saint-Antoine** (87.58) 95 rooms in a trio of historic buildings in the Old Port. 8 Rue St.-Antoine; 888/692-2211; saint-antoine.com; doubles from $–$$.

❺ **Fairmont Le Château Frontenac** (87.78) 1893 castle-style building with views of the St. Lawrence River. 1 Rue des Carrières; 800/441-1414; fairmont.com; doubles from $–$$.

CARIBBEAN, BERMUDA + THE BAHAMAS

ANGUILLA

CuisinArt Golf Resort & Spa (88.29) Six villas with 93 upgraded rooms, a 7,000-square-foot sushi restaurant, and the island's largest spa complex. Rendezvous Bay; 800/943-3210; cuisinartresort.com; doubles from $$–$$$$, including breakfast.

ANTIGUA

Curtain Bluff (91.29) Colonial-era style in 72 rooms and suites along Surf Beach; once-a-week seafood dinners are served on the sand. St. John's; 888/289-9898; curtainbluff.com; doubles from $$$–$$$$, all-inclusive.

Jumby Bay, A Rosewood Resort (88.17) The epitome of Caribbean luxury on a 300-acre island; a $28 million reconstruction in 2009 added the open-air Sense spa and Estate Homes. Jumby Bay Island; 888/767-3966; rosewoodhotels.com; doubles from $$$$–$$$$$, all-inclusive.

Sandals Grande Antigua Caribbean Village & Spa (87.72) A mega-resort on Dickenson Bay that's two properties in one: the Caribbean Grove is known for its 17 rondavels; the Mediterranean village has piazzas and suites with Italian marble. St. John's; 800/726-3257; sandals.com; doubles from $$$$$, all-inclusive, 2-night minimum.

BAHAMAS

One&Only Ocean Club (88.98) British-colonial hideaway and a Jean-Georges restaurant, plus Adam Tihany interiors in the hotel's updated Crescent Wing. Paradise Island; 888/528-7157; oneandonlyresorts.com; doubles from $$$–$$$$.

Sandals Emerald Bay (87.64) Two-year-old sprawling tropical resort that sports a Greg Norman golf course, French restaurant, and 60-slip marina for those arriving by boat. Great Exuma; 800/726-3257; sandals.com; doubles from $$$$$, all-inclusive, 2-night minimum.

BARBADOS

Sandy Lane (88.88) A Rolls-Royce Phantom airport transfer brings guests to this Palladian-style palace (a 7,500-square-foot swimming pool; tennis; jewelry boutiques) surrounded by 3 golf courses on a quiet bay. St. James; 866/444-4080; sandylane.com; doubles from $$$$$.

BERMUDA

Reefs Hotel & Club (87.93) 57 western-facing rooms on a pink-sand beach; the sunset views are unparalleled. Southampton; 800/742-2008; thereefs.com; doubles from $$–$$$, including breakfast, afternoon tea, and dinner.

BRITISH VIRGIN ISLANDS

Sugar Mill Hotel (87.20) 23-room cottage colony with alfresco stone showers; set in a former rum distillery just steps from a 200-foot private beach rimmed by tropical gardens. Tortola; 800/462-8834; sugarmillhotel.com; doubles from $$.

Rosewood Little Dix Bay (87.71) Old-world touches (including restaurant dress codes) and water activities—sailing, snorkeling—on a pristine half-mile crescent beach. Virgin Gorda; 888/767-3966; rosewoodhotels.com; doubles from $$–$$$.

CAYMAN ISLANDS

Ritz-Carlton Grand Cayman (89.76) 365-room oceanfront haven offering nature tours crafted by Jean-Michel Cousteau, a La Prairie spa, and a restaurant by chef Eric Ripert. Seven Mile Beach; 800/241-3333; ritzcarlton.com; doubles from $$$$.

JAMAICA

Couples Negril (91.21) Colorful, 234-room resort and 5 restaurants on 18 acres fronting Bloody Bay Beach. Negril; 800/268-7537; couples.com; doubles from $$–$$$, all-inclusive.

Couples Sans Souci (92.41) Couples' most intimate Caribbean hideaway: 150 rooms overlooking a cove in Ocho Rios. St. Mary; 800/268-7537; couples.com; doubles from $$–$$$$$, all-inclusive, 3-night minimum.

Couples Swept Away (92.93) 312 suites, waterskiing, pool volleyball, and even a nightclub, on 27 acres along Seven Mile Beach. Westmoreland; 800/268-7537; couples.com; doubles from $$–$$$.

Couples Tower Isle (94.33) The original Couples property is a 226-room, all-inclusive, adults-only resort with an award-winning spa. Ocho Rios; 800/268-7537; couples.com; doubles from $$–$$$.

❺ **Rockhouse Hotel** (88.19) Chic-but-casual cliffside retreat: private sundecks, a chilled-out spa, a Jamaican street-food restaurant, and great snorkeling. Negril; 876/957-4373; rockhousehotel.com; doubles from $.

NEVIS

Nisbet Plantation Beach Club (95.24) Unpretentious 36-room wicker-and-wood inn and 1778 great house on 30 acres; the Caribbean's only historic plantation inn on the beach. 800/742-6008; nisbetplantation.com; doubles from $$–$$$, including breakfast, tea, and dinner.

PUERTO RICO

Hotel El Convento (87.59) A 17th-century former convent in Old San Juan with Andalusian antiques and modern amenities. 100 Cristo St., San Juan; 800/468-2779; elconvento.com; doubles from $$.

ST. BART'S

Eden Rock – St. Barths (92.00) A 34-room, celebrity-studded hotel with an art gallery and studio and 2 open-air restaurants where ingredients are sourced from the on-site herb and vegetable garden. Baie de St. Jean; 877/563-7105; edenrockhotel.com; doubles from $$$–$$$$$.

Hotel Saint-Barth Isle de France (92.57) Beach club–style boutique hotel, a Natura Bissé spa, and 2 new villas on the island's widest stretch of sand. Baie de Flamands; 800/810-4691; isle-de-france.com; doubles from $$$–$$$$, including breakfast and airport transfers.

ST. LUCIA

Anse Chastanet Resort (88.25) Nature-centric hillside cottages in a 600-acre forest on the volcanic southwestern coast. Soufrière; 800/223-1108; ansechastanet.com; doubles from $$.

Jade Mountain (90.49) The 29 open-air suites have either a private infinity pool or whirlpool—and only 3 walls, for dramatic Piton views. Soufrière; 800/223-1108; jademountainstlucia.com; doubles from $$$$–$$$$$.

Jalousie Plantation, Sugar Beach (90.25) Beachfront bungalows on a former sugar estate, undergoing a $100 million redo before relaunching as Tides Sugar Beach in 2012. La Baie de Silence; 800/235-4300; jalousieplantation.com; doubles from $$–$$$.

Ladera Resort (92.30) 32 mountainside villas and suites open to the elements on one side; guests spend their days on boat tours, in cooking classes, and lounging by the infinity pool. Soufrière; 866/290-0978; ladera.com; doubles from $$–$$$.

TURKS AND CAICOS

Amanyara (88.00) West Indian outpost of Amanresorts—all polished concrete and terrazzo—on a marine preserve. Providenciales; 800/477-

KEY TO THE PRICE ICONS   **$** UNDER $250   **$$** $250–$499   **$$$** $500–$749   **$$$$** $750–$999   **$$$$$** $1,000 AND UP   ❺ GREAT VALUE ($250 OR LESS)

Modernist daybeds at Turks and Caicos's Grace Bay Club.

9180; amanresorts.com; doubles from $$$$$.

Gansevoort Hotel (87.75) A 91-room resort with a South Beach vibe. Grace Bay Beach; 888/844-5986; gansevoortturksandcaicos.com; doubles from $$–$$$.

Grace Bay Club (88.08) Resort complex with an adults-only wing, family villas, and a 5,157-square-foot gym and spa. Providenciales; 800/946-5757; gracebayresorts.com; doubles from $$$–$$$$.

Parrot Cay (87.85) A wellness-oriented private-island resort with feng shui–approved Asian accents and the top-notch Como Shambhala spa. Providenciales; 877/754-0726; como.bz; doubles from $$$.

Regent Palms (92.00) Five low-slung buildings on Grace Bay Beach make up the only Regent in the Americas. Perks include a new kids' club. Providenciales; 800/967-9044; regenthotels.com; doubles from $$$–$$$$.

U.S. VIRGIN ISLANDS

Ritz-Carlton (87.90) Mangrove-shrouded beach escape (infinity pool;

sushi bar; aquatic center) on 30 acres in Great Bay. St. Thomas; 800/241-3333; ritzcarlton.com; doubles from $$–$$$.

MEXICO + CENTRAL + SOUTH AMERICA

ARGENTINA

BARILOCHE

Llao Llao Hotel & Resort, Golf-Spa (88.25) 205-room lakeside lodge with alpine perks (private whirlpools; towel-warming racks) in the snowcapped Andes of Patagonia. 800/223-6800; llaollao.com.ar; doubles from $$–$$$.

BUENOS AIRES

Alvear Palace Hotel (92.58) Classic French-inspired hotel (Hermès amenities; Louis XV design elements) celebrating its 80th year. A new sister property will open nearby in Plaza San Martín in summer 2012. 1891 Avda. Alvear; 800/223-6800; alvearpalace.com; doubles from $$–$$$$.

Four Seasons Hotel (90.50) 1920 mansion and tower connected by

immaculately landscaped grounds and an herb garden, in exclusive La Recoleta. 1086/88 Calle Posadas; 800/332-3442; fourseasons.com; doubles from $$–$$$.

Palacio Duhau - Park Hyatt (94.97) Two hotels in one—a Belle Époque mansion and a sleek 17-story addition—plus an on-site art gallery and a 3,500-label wine cellar. 1661 Avda. Alvear; 877/875-4658; park.hyatt.com; doubles from $$–$$$.

Sofitel Buenos Aires Arroyo (87.25) Neoclassical French high-rise (the city's first skyscraper) with Art Deco interiors from Pierre-Yves Rochon and a refreshed Le Sud restaurant. 841 Calle Arroyo; 800/763-4835; sofitel.com; doubles from $$.

MENDOZA

Park Hyatt (91.43) A 7-story whitewashed structure on Plaza Independencia, in a noted wine region along the Andes. 877/875-4658; park.hyatt.com; doubles from $$.

BELIZE

AMBERGRIS CAY

⑤ **Victoria House** (92.17) Relaxed island resort of 7 thatched-roof casitas (plus plantation rooms and suites) and 2 pools; the best jumping-off point for exploring the world's second-largest barrier reef. 800/247-5159; victoria-house.com; doubles from $.

CHILE

EASTER ISLAND

Posada de Mike Rapu / Explora Rapa Nui (95.47) 2007 local wood, stone, and glass LEED-certified lodge 2,300 miles off Chile's coast; excursions include guided visits to the *moai* stone quarries and treks to nearby volcanoes. 866/750-6699; explora.com; doubles from $$$$$, all-inclusive, 3-night minimum.

SANTIAGO

Grand Hyatt (87.27) 310 stylish rooms and suites, a Thai restaurant, and a tri-level spa in the quiet residential district of Las Condes. 4601 Avda. Presidente Kennedy; 800/233-1234; hyatt.com; doubles from $$.

Ritz-Carlton (88.11) 205-room property aimed at business travelers in the chic El Golf neighborhood, with a new tapas restaurant by Sergi Arola and a hot-spot bar frequented by

locals. 15 Calle El Alcalde; 800/241-3333; ritzcarlton.com; doubles from $$.

COLOMBIA

CARTAGENA

Sofitel Cartagena Santa Clara (88.47) The Old City's preeminent luxury hotel, in a 17th-century former convent; the new French restaurant pours more than 250 standout bottles. 39-29 Calle del Torno; 800/763-4835; sofitel.com; doubles from $$–$$$.

COSTA RICA

GUANACASTE

Four Seasons Resort Costa Rica at Peninsula Papagayo (89.68) Hillside resort with all the trimmings (2 beaches, 3 pools, verandas, and a spa) surrounded by a tropical dry forest. 800/332-3442; fourseasons.com; doubles from $$–$$$.

JW Marriott Guanacaste Resort & Spa (88.17) Three-year-old 310-room colonial beachfront property, a quick drive from the jungle for ziplining and mountain hikes. 800/228-9290; jwmarriott.com; doubles from $$.

GUATEMALA

ANTIGUA

⑤ **Hotel Museo Casa Santo Domingo** (90.36) 16th-century convent turned hotel, colonial-art museum, and archaeological center; the renovated spa will reopen in July. 502/7820-1220; casasantodomingo.com.gt; doubles from $.

SOLOLÁ

⑤ **Hotel Atitlán** (87.24) Former coffee plantation in the Guatemalan highlands with 140 lakeside rooms and volcano vistas. 502/7762-1441; hotelatitlan.com; doubles from $.

MEXICO

CANCÚN

⑤ **Ritz-Carlton** (90.80) The brand's only Mexican property; a 362-room retreat with a 1,200-foot strip of beachfront, plus tequila tastings and cooking lessons. 36 Retorno del Rey, Zona Hotelera, 800/241-3333; ritzcarlton.com; doubles from $–$$.

Royal Cancún (90.35) A Mediterranean-style, adults-only

retreat; hammocks and showers for two lure honeymooners. Km 11.5, Kukulcan Blvd.; 800/760-0944; realresorts.com; doubles from $$$–$$$$, all-inclusive.

LOS CABOS

⑤ Casa Dorada Los Cabos Resort & Spa (88.21) Hip new suites-only spread on popular Médano Beach, a short walk from boutiques and restaurants. Cabo San Lucas; 866/448-0151; casadorada.com; doubles from $–$$.

Esperanza, an Auberge Resort (92.21) 57 spacious casitas with verandas and infinity-edge hot tubs, overlooking 2 private coves (the place for sunrise yoga). Punta Ballena; 866/311-2226; esperanzaresort.com; doubles from $$$–$$$$$.

Las Ventanas al Paraíso, A Rosewood Resort (91.77) 71-suite beach hideaway and a just-reopened spa set beneath a canopy of 45 palms. San José del Cabo; 888/767-3966; lasventanas.com; doubles from $$$.

One&Only Palmilla (93.22) 172-room resort with a boutique-hotel sensibility, 2 restaurants by Jean-Georges Vongerichten, and superb butler service, on a private beach dotted with shaded daybeds. San José del Cabo; 866/829-2977; oneandonly resorts.com; doubles from $$$.

MEXICO CITY

Four Seasons Hotel México, D.F. (92.00) Colonial-style urban getaway with 240 large rooms on a promenade near Chapultepec Park. 500 Paseo de la Reforma; 800/332-3442; four seasons.com; doubles from $$–$$$.

PUNTA MITA

⑤ Four Seasons Resort (89.94) 173 rooms, 4 restaurants, and 2 golf courses on an isthmus near Puerto Vallarta. Kids and teens stay busy in the game room. 800/332-3442; four seasons.com; doubles from $$–$$$.

RIVIERA MAYA

Excellence Riviera Cancún (90.67) Mediterranean-style 440-room resort suited for active types (jogging trails; tennis; Pilates) on the Riviera Maya. Km 324, Carr. Federal 307; 866/540-2585; excellence-resorts.com; doubles from $$–$$$.

Maroma Resort & Spa (90.22) 65 rooms and suites, 1 villa, a stunning spa, and a new tequila and mezcal bar line a powder-white stretch of sand between Cancún and Playa del Carmen. Solidaridad; 866/454-9351; maromahotel.com; doubles from $$–$$$, including breakfast.

Royal Hideaway Playacar (87.50) Traditional accents (Mexican art; lattice-wood headboards) at an adults-only beach resort 10 minutes from downtown Playa del Carmen. Playacar; 800/999-9182; royal hideaway.com; doubles from $$$–$$$$, all-inclusive.

SAN MIGUEL DE ALLENDE

⑤ Casa de Sierra Nevada (90.13) A jewel among the luxury hotel scene, with 37 rooms (some with stone fireplaces) divided among 6 Spanish-colonial mansions. 800/701-1561; casa desierranevada.com; doubles from $.

ZIHUATANEJO

La Casa Que Canta (90.53) 25-suite adobe hideaway and an ocean-fed saltwater pool above Zihuatanejo Bay. 888/523-5050; lacasaquecanta. com; doubles from $$.

PERU

CUZCO

Hotel Monasterio (91.78) 126 elegant, individually designed rooms around 3 courtyards in a converted 16th-century monastery. 136 Calle Palacio, Plazoleta Nazarenas; 800/237-1236; orient-express.com; doubles from $$$, including breakfast.

LIMA

JW Marriott Hotel (87.68) Eye-catching glass tower by Arquitectonica—with ergonomic desk chairs and a new ceviche lounge—situated on cliffs above the Pacific in picturesque Miraflores. 615 Avda. Malecón de la Reserva; 800/228-9290; jwmarriott.com; doubles from $$.

MACHU PICCHU

Inkaterra Machu Picchu Pueblo Hotel (93.47) A 12-acre retreat (85 terra-cotta-roofed casitas; an orchid garden) in the cloud forest below the ruins. 800/442-5042; inkaterra.com; doubles from $$$$, including breakfast, dinner, and excursions.

URUGUAY

CARMELO

⑤ Four Seasons Resort (95.20) 20 bungalows, 24 suites, and an Asian-influenced spa on a beach nestled between a eucalyptus forest and the Río de la Plata, all just a 3-hour trip north of Buenos Aires. Km 262, Ruta 21; 800/332-3442; fourseasons.com; doubles from $–$$.

Pouring a cocktail at Le Bar du Plaza, inside the Hôtel Plaza Athénée, in Paris.

EUROPE

AUSTRIA

SALZBURG

Hotel Goldener Hirsch, a Luxury Collection Hotel (88.51) Rustic-chic, 69-room property filled with 15th-century antiques, near Mozart's former residence in Old Town. 37 Getreidegasse; 800/325-3589; goldenerhirschsalzburg.com; doubles from $$–$$$$.

Hotel Sacher (87.27) An 1866 hotel on the Salzach River, featuring live piano music every evening and windows that look out onto the historic city center. 5-7 Schwarzstrasse; 43-662/889-770; sacher.com; doubles from $$–$$$.

VIENNA

Grand Hotel Wien (89.71) 1870 food-focused property (3 acclaimed restaurants, including the city's most authentic sushi bar) near the Kohlmarkt; 30 of the 250 rooms have been made over. 9 Kärntner Ring; 43-1/515-80-1700; grandhotelwien.com; doubles from $$–$$$.

Hotel Bristol, a Luxury Collection Hotel (89.58) Grand 19th-century hotel next to the State Opera with lavish fin de siècle interiors and Restaurant Korso, for Austrian venison or Wiener schnitzel. 1 Kärntner Ring; 800/325-3589; bristolvienna.com; doubles from $$–$$$$$.

Hotel Imperial, a Luxury Collection Hotel (91.50) 1863 palace built for the prince of Württemberg on the historic Ringstrasse; 17 of the 138 traditional rooms were refurbished in 2011. 16 Kärntner Ring; 800/325-3589; hotelimperial.com; doubles from $$$–$$$$$.

Hotel Sacher Wien (90.58) Belle Époque property renovated by Pierre-Yves Rochon opposite the opera house. The famous Sacher torte is a must. 4 Philharmon-ikerstrasse; 43-1/514-560; sacher. com; doubles from $$$–$$$$.

BELGIUM

BRUSSELS

Hotel Amigo (88.70) Light-filled

Rocco Forte hotel near the Grand Place. Designer Olga Polizzi decorated the interiors with classic and modern art, including works by Belgian-born René Magritte. 1-3 Rue de l'Amigo; 888/667-9477; hotelamigo.com; doubles from $$-$$$$.

CZECH REPUBLIC

PRAGUE

Four Seasons Hotel (90.00) Four architecturally distinct buildings on the east bank of the Vltava River; the Michelin-starred Mediterranean Allegro will become a new Italian restaurant this year. 2A/1098 Veleslavinova; 800/332-3442; fourseasons.com; doubles from $$$.

DENMARK

COPENHAGEN

Hotel d'Angleterre (89.87) 250-year-old legend on King's Square, completely overhauled and reopened in spring 2012 with 91 enlarged rooms and 4 new restaurants and bars. 34 Kongens Nytorv; 45/3312-0095; dangleterre.dk; doubles from $$$.

ENGLAND

BATH

Royal Crescent Hotel (89.83) Cluster of 18th-century buildings (including a coach house turned spa) overlooking the Crescent's lawns, surrounded by Georgian-era residences. 44-1225/823-333; royalcrescent.co.uk; doubles from $$-$$$, including breakfast.

LONDON

Brown's Hotel (88.00) 11 Georgian town houses in Mayfair restored by Rocco Forte that combine historic (Churchill and Kipling were guests) and interiors with modern art on display. Albemarle St.; 888/667-9477; brownshotel.com; doubles from $$-$$$$.

Chesterfield Mayfair Hotel (88.44) Intimate, family-run hotel near Green Park, with subtly themed rooms (Savile Row; African savanna) and a popular chocolate-centered afternoon tea. 35 Charles St.; 877/955-1515; chesterfieldmayfair.com; doubles from $$-$$$.

Dukes (87.52) Discreet 90-room property on a quiet cul-de-sac steps from Green Park and St. James's Palace, now with 11 refurbished suites, a Nigel Mendhem restaurant, and a champagne lounge. 36 St. James's Place; 800/381-4702; dukeshotel.com; doubles from $$-$$$.

41 (87.58) Black-and-white interiors and the air of a private club (a library filled with leather-bound books; lounge-side canapés), steps from Buckingham Palace. 41 Buckingham Palace Rd.; 877/955-1515; 41hotel.com; doubles from $$.

Four Seasons Hotel London at Park Lane (88.46) 11-story property remodeled in 2011 by Pierre-Yves Rochon; the glass-walled rooftop spa has panoramic views of iconic sites such as Big Ben. Hamilton Place, Park Lane; 800/332-3442; fourseasons.com; doubles from $$-$$$$.

The Goring (90.18) Family-owned hotel near Buckingham Palace where Kate Middleton slept before her wedding; interiors are by noted British decorators. Beeston Place; 800/525-4800; thegoring.com; doubles from $$-$$$.

The Lanesborough (91.62) 93-room Regency-style building, Cognac bar, and cigar lounge in Knightsbridge. The new 4,000-square-foot Lanesborough Suite by Alberto Pinto comes with access to a chauffeured Rolls-Royce. Hyde Park Corner; 800/999-1828; lanesborough.com; doubles from $$$$.

The Langham (92.32) 1865 landmark restored to its Victorian grandeur; big-name additions include the first-in-Europe Chuan Spa and a David Collins–designed restaurant. 1C Portland Place, Regent St.; 800/588-9141; langhamhotels.co.uk; doubles from $$-$$$$.

Mandarin Oriental Hyde Park (90.71) Former Victorian gentleman's club with a restaurant by Daniel Boulud and the Michelin-starred Dinner by Heston Blumenthal, plus a state-of-the-art spa. 66 Knightsbridge; 800/526-6566; mandarinoriental.com; doubles from $$-$$$$$.

Milestone Hotel (92.35) 62 rooms in a red-brick Victorian with charming touches (picnic-basket lunches;

English sweets at turndown), opposite Kensington Palace. 1 Kensington Court; 877/955-1515; milestonehotel.com; doubles from $$-$$$.

The Savoy (90.40) Venerable Thames-front property that houses Pierre-Yves Rochon interiors and the Gordon Ramsay–managed Savoy Grill, now with new chef Andy Cook. Strand; 800/257-7544; fairmont.com; doubles from $$-$$$$$.

Soho Hotel (87.77) 91-room Tim and Kit Kemp property with cheeky touches (retro Tivoli radios; bright pink armchairs) and luxurious amenities (a personal trainer; Frette linens). 4 Richmond Mews; 888/559-5508; sohohotel.com; doubles from $$.

Stafford London by Kempinski (94.40) Refined, recently updated town house behind Green Park with an 8,000-bottle, 17th-century wine cellar and a new rustic restaurant, the Lyttelton. St. James's Place; 800/426-3135; kempinski.com; doubles from $$-$$$$.

FRANCE

BURGUNDY

🟢 **Hôtel Le Cep** (89.00) Cluster of 14th- to 16th-century buildings housing 64 rooms (each named after a *grand cru* wine) and a traditional Burgundian restaurant that earned a Michelin star in 2010. Beaune; 800/688-0414; hotel-cep-beaune.com; doubles from $.

CÔTE D'AZUR

Château de la Chèvre d'Or (88.33) 37 individually designed rooms, a Michelin 2-starred restaurant, and a private garden on a cliff above the Mediterranean. Èze Village; 33-4/92-10-66-66; chevredor.com; doubles from $$.

Château Eza (91.20) 17th-century hotel with 11 rooms (stone balconies; travertine bathrooms) and a Michelin-starred restaurant built into the rock walls of the medieval town. Èze Village; 33-4/93-41-12-24; chateaueza.com; doubles from $$-$$$.

🟢 **Hôtel Le Negresco** (87.82) A national monument noted for its pink dome overlooking Nice's Baie des Anges. La Rotonde, a carousel-themed restaurant, has an expanded terrace. 37 Promenade des Anglais, Nice;

33-4/93-16-64-00; hotel-negresco-nice.com; doubles from $-$$.

La Colombe d'Or (87.73) A favorite for the creative set: this inn where artists gathered in the 1920's is a charming 25-room hotel filled with works by Matisse, Picasso, Calder, and Miró. St.-Paul-de-Vence; 33-4/93-32-80-02; la-colombe-dor.com; doubles from $$.

LOIRE VALLEY

🟢 **Domaine des Hauts de Loire** (91.05) 31-room 19th-century former hunting lodge on 178 forested acres between Blois and Amboise. Onzain; 33-2/54-20-72-57; domainehautsloire.com; doubles from $.

PARIS

Four Seasons Hotel George V (92.09) Crystal chandeliers, cutting-edge floral designs, and private verandas—plus a Michelin 2-starred restaurant—in an elegant 1928 icon. 31 Ave. George V; 800/332-3442; fourseasons.com; doubles from $$$$$.

Hospes Lancaster (90.35) Chic, 57-room hotel set in a 19th-century mansion near the Champs-Élysées that has lured luminaries from Greta Garbo to Jeremy Irons. Interiors were renovated in 2012. 7 Rue de Berri; 33-1/40-76-40-76; hotel-lancaster.fr; doubles from $$$.

Hôtel de Crillon (91.91) Louis XV–commissioned 1758 palace; Les Ambassadeurs restaurant, set in a restored ballroom, was awarded its first Michelin star in 2011. 10 Place de la Concorde; 33-1/44-71-15-00; crillon.com; doubles from $$$$-$$$$$.

Hôtel Le Bristol (91.00) 1925 property beloved by fashion photographers and 1960's film stars; updated with the Haussmannian Matignon wing, the Faubourg 114 brasserie, and a La Prairie spa. 112 Rue du Faubourg St.-Honoré; 33-1/53-43-43-00; lebristolparis.com; doubles from $$$$$.

Hôtel Le Meurice (90.64) Dorchester Collection hotel with Louis XVI–style interiors and public spaces by Philippe Starck. 228 Rue de Rivoli; 800/650-1842; lemeurice.com; doubles from $$$$-$$$$$.

Hôtel Plaza Athénée (93.63) A Haussmann-era Dorchester Collection hotel—fresh from a 2011 renovation—home to a Michelin 3-starred Alain Ducasse restaurant, 35,000-bottle wine cellar, and Eiffel Tower views. 25 Ave. Montaigne; 800/650-1842; plaza-atthenee-paris.com; doubles from $$$$$.

Park Hyatt Paris-Vendôme (90.00) Palace hotel defined by sleek interiors—a daring departure from its more traditional neighbors—just off Place Vendôme. A new hair salon that remains open 24/7 draws the city's style set. 5 Rue de la Paix; 800/233-1234; park.hyatt.com; doubles from $$$$$.

Ritz Paris (91.15) Lavish, 159-room manse built by César Ritz in 1898 and filled with gilded touches such as the Greek-style columned pool and swan-shaped faucets. 15 Place Vendôme; 33-1/43-16-30-30; ritzparis.com; doubles from $$$$$.

REIMS

Domaine Les Crayères (88.73) Impeccable 1904 château on 18 acres in the heart of the Champagne-Ardenne region; the concierge arranges access to the region's best cellars (Pommery, Taittinger, Veuve Clicquot). 33-3/26-24-90-00; lescrayeres.com; doubles from $$$.

GERMANY

BADEN-BADEN

Brenners Park-Hotel & Spa (93.00) 1874 resort, Michelin 2-starred restaurant, and prestigious 2,500-square-foot medical spa complex in a town famous for its thermal springs. 49-7221/9000; brenners.com; doubles from $$.

BERLIN

Hotel Adlon Kempinski (89.56) Century-old grande dame and modern addition, across from the Brandenburg Gate; popular with a younger crowd for its summer Moët & Chandon champagne bar on Pariser Platz. 77 Unter den Linden; 800/426-3135; kempinski.com; doubles from $$.

⑤ Kempinski Hotel Bristol (87.47) White-gloved service and an endless breakfast buffet in a commanding, 250,000-square-foot semicircular structure on one of the city's main thoroughfares. 27 Kurfürstendamm;

800/426-3135; kempinski.com; doubles from $–$$$.

MUNICH

Hotel Vier Jahreszeiten Kempinski (87.41) 153-year-old Neoclassical-style landmark undergoing a $20 million-plus makeover with a restored stained-glass dome; edgy accents (translucent chairs; oversize photos); and a light-filled lobby that channels a bygone era. 17 Maximilianstrasse; 800/426-3135; kempinski.com; doubles from $$–$$$.

Mandarin Oriental (91.50) 73 Asian-inspired rooms and suites in a Neo-Renaissance former opera house; wellness amenities include a rooftop pool, an updated fitness center, and a fleet of Mercedes-Benz bicycles. 1 Neuturmstrasse; 800/526-6566; mandarinoriental.com; doubles from $$$–$$$$.

ROTHENBURG OB DER TAUBER

⑤ Hotel Eisenhut (88.62) 78 rooms in a series of 15th- and 16th-century mansions in the Bavarian town's medieval walled center; traditional Franconian dishes are served on the terrace and in the beer garden. 49-9861/7050; eisenhut.com; doubles from $–$$.

GREECE

ATHENS

Hotel Grande Bretagne, a Luxury Collection Hotel (89.92) Landmark 1874 property that overlooks the Acropolis and Mount Lycabettus (the best views are from the rooftop bar and pool). Vas. Georgiou A1; 800/325-3589; grandebretagne.gr; doubles from $$–$$$$.

King George Palace (88.13) Glitzy Neoclassical hotel just off Constitution Square. The 102 rooms feature raw-silk bedspreads and Murano chandeliers; the breakfast buffet is the most famous in town. 3 Vas. Georgiou A; 30-210/322-2210; classicalhotels.com; doubles from $$–$$$.

SANTORINI

Katikies Hotel (93.07) White-on-white property seemingly sculpted into the Aegean cliffs; the nightly wine tasting offers views of the twin infinity pools and volcanic caldera. Oia; 30-

22860/71401; katikies.com; doubles from $$$–$$$$, including breakfast.

HUNGARY

BUDAPEST

Four Seasons Hotel Gresham Palace (92.90) Art Nouveau masterpiece (gold mosaic towers; turn-of-the-century stained-glass portraits) at the base of the Chain Bridge, complete with a new Omorovicza spa menu and open-air terrace at Gresham restaurant. 5-6 Szechenyi Tér; 800/332-3442; fourseasons.com; doubles from $$.

⑤ Kempinski Hotel Corvinus (90.82) 359-room, glass-and-granite structure with 2 restaurants—Restaurant Giardino, serving a popular Sunday brunch, and the first outpost of Nobu in Central Europe—within walking distance of St. Stephen's Basilica. 7-8 Erzsébet Tér; 800/426-3135; kempinski.com; doubles from $–$$.

IRELAND

COUNTY CLARE

Dromoland Castle (89.79) Baronial 16th century estate in a fairy-tale setting (lily ponds; rose garden; clay shooting range) with a parkland golf course. Newmarket-on-Fergus; 800/346-7007; dromoland.ie; doubles from $$–$$$.

COUNTY KERRY

Park Hotel Kenmare (92.21) Classic 46-room Victorian hotel overlooking Kenmare Bay; the Samas Spa, one of Ireland's top wellness centers, now offers Sisley of Paris treatments. Kenmare; 800/525-4800; parkkenmare.com; doubles from $$$, including breakfast.

COUNTY LIMERICK

Adare Manor Hotel & Golf Resort (87.74) 1832 neo-Gothic château and 62 antiques-filled rooms amid a Robert Trent Jones Sr.–designed golf course and French formal gardens of boxwood parterres and lavender. Adare; 800/462-3273; adaremanor.com; doubles from $$–$$$.

COUNTY MAYO

⑤ Ashford Castle (89.95) Medieval crenellated castle on 350 acres along

the banks of Lough Corrib. A newly added 50-room country house (pillow-top mattresses; heated bathroom floors) debuted in July. Cong; 800/346-7007; ashford.ie; doubles from $–$$, including breakfast.

DUBLIN

Four Seasons Hotel (89.25) 197-room red-brick property in an affluent suburb just south of the city. The 2 bars suit different tastes: The Bar serves whiskey; white-on-white Ice is for wine and tapas. Simmonscourt Rd.; 800/332-3442; fourseasons.com; doubles from $$, including breakfast.

The Merrion (88.57) Four Georgian houses (and a Michelin-starred restaurant) near the National Gallery; the hotel's art collection houses works by 20th-century Irish painters. Upper Merrion St.; 800/223-6800; merrionhotel.com; doubles from $$$–$$$$$.

The Shelbourne (87.47) Historic Georgian building—Ireland's first constitution was drafted here in 1922—opposite St. Stephen's Green; a new on-site history museum and Tethra spa open this spring. 27 St. Stephen's Green; 888/236-2427; theshelbourne.ie; doubles from $$.

ITALY

AMALFI COAST

Grand Hotel Excelsior Vittoria (88.28) Three adjoining brick buildings above the Bay of Naples, owned and operated by the same family since 1834, just 2 minutes from the Marina Piccola di Sorrento. Sorrento; 800/325-8541; exvitt.it; doubles from $$–$$$, including breakfast.

Hotel Caruso (94.75) 11th-century palace with an infinity pool, terraced gardens, and classic-celebrity cachet (Jackie Kennedy; Humphrey Bogart). Ravello; 800/237-1236; hotelcaruso.com; doubles from $$$$–$$$$$.

Hotel Santa Caterina (90.18) 67-room seafront villa and cliffside saltwater pool (once the hideaway of Liz Taylor and Richard Burton) surrounded by lemon orchards. Amalfi; 39-08/987-1012; hotelsantacaterina.it; doubles from $$–$$$$, including breakfast.

Il San Pietro di Positano (90.58) Cliff-hanging architectural wonder located high above the Amalfi Coast, with 59 rooms and a private sandy beach reached via elevator. Positano; 800/735-2478; ilsanpietro.it; doubles from $$$-$$$$.

Le Sirenuse (92.68) Set in the 1951 former summer residence of the Marchesi Sersale, this 59-room gem hotel has the Neopolitan La Sponda restaurant and dazzling views of Positano and the Mediterranean. Guests can explore the coastline from the hotel's vintage wooden speedboat. Positano; 800/223-6800; sirenuse.it; doubles from $$-$$$.

Palazzo Sasso (92.96) Aristocratic 12th-century palazzo with 43 well-appointed rooms (Vietri tile floors; Bulgari amenities), a Michelin-starred restaurant, and a heated pool with an underwater window for views of the sea. Ravello; 39-089/818-181; palazzosasso.com; doubles from $$-$$$, including breakfast.

ASOLO

Hotel Villa Cipriani (93.75) 31-room country escape—the former residence of Robert and Elizabeth Barrett Browning—on a hilltop for the ultimate in privacy. 800/223-5652; villaciprianiasolo.com; doubles from $$-$$$, including breakfast.

CAPRI

Grand Hotel Quisisana (90.86) Palatial 19th-century hotel and spa—with Capri's only hammam and the see-and-be-seen Quisi Bar—surrounded by palms and pine trees near Piazza Umberto. 800/223-6800; quisisana.com; doubles from $$.

FLORENCE

Four Seasons Hotel Firenze (91.51) A 1472 palace near the Duomo with 160 impeccable rooms, frescoed halls, and discreet service, next to a centuries-old, 11-acre private park. 99 Borgo Pinti; 800/332-3442; fourseasons.com; doubles from $$-$$$$.

The glass cupola above the reception area at the Four Seasons Hotel Gresham Palace, in Budapest.

ⓢ **Hotel Bernini** (87.33) Gilded 15th-century manse with North African details (Moroccan lanterns; oversize glass urns) across from the Palazzo Vecchio. 29 Piazza San Firenze; 39-055/288-621; duetorrihotels.com; doubles from $-$$$, including breakfast.

Hotel Helvetia & Bristol (88.71) 67-room hotel featuring 17th-century antiques and Tuscan cooking classes, close to the 1489 Palazzo Strozzi in the *centro storico*. 2 Via dei Pescioni; 39-055/26651; royaldemeure.com; doubles from $$-$$$.

ⓢ **Hotel Lungarno** (87.90) Handsome 73-room medieval building filled with more than 400 works of art—including a Picasso sketch—on the Arno's south bank. The new Lounge Bar Picteau serves house-made ganaches and pralines during afternoon tea. 14 Borgo San Jacopo; 39-055/27261; lungarnohotels.com; doubles from $-$$, including breakfast.

Hotel Savoy (89.82) Ferragamo-owned 19th-century palazzo designed by Olga Polizzi (complete with quirky photos of shoes), on café-lined Piazza della Repubblica, just steps from the Duomo. 7 Piazza della Repubblica; 888/667-9477; roccofortehotels.com; doubles from $$-$$$$.

St. Regis (formerly the Grand Hotel) (88.69) Newly rebranded 100-room Renaissance palace—built in 1432 by the architect of the Duomo Santa Maria del Fiore—illuminated by the original crystal chandeliers. French doors overlook the Arno. 1 Piazza Ognissanti; 800/325-3589; stregis. com; doubles from $$-$$$$$.

Westin Excelsior (90.48) A 300-label wine cellar and a new Mediterranean rooftop restaurant, plus 171 rooms and the sleep-inducing Heavenly beds, in a 15th-century palace near the Ponte Vecchio. 3 Piazza Ognissanti; 800/228-3000; westin. com; doubles from $$-$$$$$.

LAKE COMO

Grand Hotel Villa Serbelloni (90.53) 19th-century villa on a promontory that stretches out to the center of Lake Como; evenings are filled with music from a piano, violin, and bass trio. Bellagio; 800/860-8672; villaserbelloni.com; doubles from $$$, including breakfast.

Villa d'Este (92.75) 1568 waterfront estate built for a Cardinal, plus a

smaller, 27-room Queens Residence, all on 25 acres of parkland along Lake Como; resort-like amenities include a Turkish bath, squash court, and 3 pools. Cernobbio; 800/223-6800; villadeste.com; doubles from $$$-$$$$, including breakfast.

MILAN

Four Seasons Hotel (89.60) 118-room hotel in a 15th-century former convent, near Milan's best shopping on Via Gesgrave; a new 8,600-square-foot spa and fitness center opens this spring. 6/8 Via Gesù; 800/332-3442; fourseasons.com; doubles from $$$-$$$$.

Park Hyatt (93.05) Modern, 108-room property in a classic building close to the Piazza Duomo and Teatro alla Scala opera house; explore the city on 2 wheels thanks to a complimentary bike-rental progam. 1 Via Tommaso Grossi; 877/875-4658; park.hyatt.com; doubles from $$$-$$$$$.

PORTOFINO

Hotel Splendido (93.33) A flower-filled hillside villa (a monastery in the 14th and 15th centuries) with views of the bay. 800/223-6800; hotelsplendido.com; doubles from $$$$$, including breakfast.

ROME

Hotel de Russie (91.11) Stylish 1814 palazzo on the fashionable Via del Babuino lined with Mapplethorpe photographs and known for its terraced gardens and standout team of concierges. 9 Via del Babuino; 888/667-9477; roccofortehotels.com; doubles from $$$-$$$$.

Hotel Hassler (89.86) Turn-of-the-century palace hotel at the top of the Spanish Steps; 6 rooms in the Il Vicolletto wing now boast 21st-century amenities, including complimentary Wi-Fi and iPod docking stations. 6 Piazza Trinità dei Monti; 800/223-6800; hotelhassler roma.com; doubles from $$-$$$$.

Rome Cavalieri, a Waldorf Astoria Hotel (87.51) 1960 property on the highest hill in Rome, with massive rooms and the city's largest pool, all set in a 15-acre private park. 101 Via A. Cadlolo; 800/445-8667; romecavalieri. com; doubles from $$-$$$$$.

TAORMINA

Grand Hotel Timeo (87.68) The first hotel to be built in Taormina, this 19th-century residence that once belonged to Sicilian nobility overlooks the bay and is situated next to a Greek theater. New owner Orient-Express added a wellness area and its own Turkish bath. 800/237-1236; orient-express.com; doubles from $$$, including breakfast.

VENICE

Bauer Il Palazzo (89.57) Peaceful, 72-room palazzo turned boutique hotel in the heart of Venice with perks such as a rooftop whirlpool and its own Grand Canal berth. 1459 San Marco; 800/223-6800; ilpalazzovenezia.com; doubles from $$$–$$$$$.

Hotel Cipriani (89.88) Giuseppe Cipriani's magical getaway—2 historic palazzi, a 1950's-era main building, an Olympic-size pool, and a lagoon-side restaurant—across the canal from San Marco on Giudecca island. 10 Giudecca; 800/237-1236; hotelcipriani.com; doubles from $$$$$, including breakfast.

Hotel Danieli, a Luxury Collection Hotel (88.77) A trio of palaces from the 14th, 19th, and 20th centuries, with 225 rooms (some refurbished by Jacques Garcia) overlooking the Venice lagoon. 4196 Riva degli Schiavoni; 800/325-3589; danielihotelvenice.com; doubles from $$–$$$$$.

Hotel Gritti Palace, a Luxury Collection Hotel (88.68) 16th-century Renaissance palace on the banks of the Grand Canal, closed through March 2013 for a major renovation. 2467 Campo Santa Maria del Giglio; 800/325-3589; hotelgrittipalace venice.com; doubles from $$–$$$$$.

⊖ San Clemente Palace (90.25) Venetian history meets resort charms at this converted 18th-century monastery with an outdoor pool and 2 tennis courts on San Clemente Island. 1 Isola di San Clemente; 39-041/244-5001; sanclementepalacevenice.com; doubles from $–$$, including breakfast.

MONACO

MONTE CARLO

Hôtel de Paris (92.29) Recently renovated marble-and-gilt Belle Époque structure on the Place du Casino that is home to Alain Ducasse's Louis XV restaurant. Place du Casino; 800/223-6800; hoteldeparismonte carlo.com; doubles from $$$–$$$$$.

THE NETHERLANDS

AMSTERDAM

InterContinental Amstel (90.29) Grand 1867 hotel on the edge of the Amstel River, a short walk from the Rijksmuseum. 1 Professor Tulpplein; 800/327-0200; ichotels group.com; doubles from $$–$$$$$.

PORTUGAL

LISBON

Four Seasons Hotel Ritz (92.00) Midcentury hotel and rooftop fitness center just 5 minutes from Old Town. 88 Rua Rodrigo da Fonseca; 800/332-3442; fourseasons.com; doubles from $$$, including breakfast.

Olissippo Lapa Palace (93.87) A 19th-century villa surrounded by gardens in the embassy district. 4 Rua do Pau de Bandeira; 351-21/394-9494; olissippohotels.com; doubles from $$$, including breakfast.

SCOTLAND

AYRSHIRE

⊖ Turnberry Resort, a Luxury Collection Hotel (93.88) 150 rooms (40 recently updated) in a massive estate on a coastal bluff; 2 championship golf courses and a 19th-century lighthouse overlook the bucolic scene. Turnberry; 800/325-3589; turnberry resort.co.uk; doubles from $–$$.

EDINBURGH

⊖ The Balmoral (88.67) Edwardian hotel topped by a 195-foot clock tower next to Waverly Station. 1 Princes St.; 888/667-9477; roccofortehotels.com; doubles from $–$$$.

ST. ANDREWS

Old Course Hotel, Golf Resort & Spa (91.58) The only hotel on the world's oldest golf course, with touches both classic (striped wallpaper) and contemporary (23 suites by Jacques Garcia). 44-133/447-4371; oldcourse hotel.co.uk; doubles from $$–$$$, including breakfast.

SPAIN

BARCELONA

Hotel Arts (87.79) Ritz-Carlton–managed hotel in a 44-story tower rising above the seafront at Port

Olympic. 19-21 Carr. de la Marina; 800/241-3333; ritzcarlton.com; doubles from $$–$$$.

MADRID

Hotel Ritz (88.95) 1910 grande dame near Paseo del Prado with lavish Belle Époque style (soaring ceilings; French antiques). 5 Plaza de la Lealtad; 800/241-3333; ritzcarlton. com; doubles from $$$.

SEVILLE

Hotel Alfonso XIII, a Luxury Collection Hotel (87.91) 1928 Neo-Moorish property reopened after a $22 million renovation. 2 Calle San Fernando; 800/325-3589; hotel-alfonsoxiii-seville.com; doubles from $$–$$$$$.

SWEDEN

STOCKHOLM

Grand Hotel (90.46) Waterfront icon—the site of the first Nobel Prize ceremony—noted for culinary achievement (the Mathias Dahlgren dining room was awarded 2 Michelin stars in 2011 and his bistro earned 1) and its 14,000-bottle wine cellar. 8 S. Blasieholmshamnen; 800/327-0200; grandhotel.se; doubles from $$–$$$.

SWITZERLAND

ZURICH

Park Hyatt (88.21) Contemporary 2004 building with modern art (Sol LeWitt; Heinz Mack), in the financial district. 21 Beethoven-Strasse; 877/875-4658; park.hyatt. com; doubles from $$$–$$$$$.

TURKEY

ISTANBUL

Çirağan Palace Kempinski (90.11) Former sultan's palace with a contemporary annex and organic

The Majorelle Suite at La Mamounia, in Marrakesh.

restaurant on the European shore of the Bosporus. 32 Çirağan Cad.; 800/426-3135; kempinski.com; doubles from $$$.

Four Seasons Hotel Istanbul at Sultanahmet (90.00) Over-the-top restored Neoclassical prison in the Old City; the leafy terrace looks onto Hagia Sophia, around the corner. 1 Tevkifhane Sk.; 800/332-3442; fourseasons.com; doubles from $$–$$$$.

Four Seasons Hotel Istanbul at the Bosphorus (90.40) 19th-century building with a 23,000-square-foot spa (hammam; skylit indoor pool). 28 Çirağan Cad.; 800/332-3442; fourseasons.com; doubles from $$$.

❺ **Hilton** (87.73) 499-room compound (7 restaurants, tennis courts, and a massive pool) surrounded by lush gardens in the heart of the city. Cumhuriyet Cad.; 800/445-8667; hilton.com; doubles from $–$$$$.

Ritz-Carlton (88.00) Ottoman-style skyscraper on a hill near Taksim Square and the city's cruise port; all 244 rooms were refurbished last year. 15 Asker Ocaği Cad.; 800/241-3333; ritzcarlton.com; doubles from $$.

AFRICA + THE MIDDLE EAST

BOTSWANA

CHOBE NATIONAL PARK

Savute Elephant Camp (88.63) 12 tents set along the Savute Channel, a gathering place for Kalahari elephants now that water is flowing again after 30 years. 800/237-1236; savuteelephantcamp.com; doubles from $$$$$.

MOREMI GAME RESERVE

Mombo Camp and Little Mombo Camp (94.82) Two groups of tents with plunge pools and unshaded decks for prime bird-watching and rhino-spotting, all linked by raised walkways on an Okavango Delta floodplain. 27-11/807-1800; wilderness-safaris.com; doubles from $$$$$, all-inclusive.

OKAVANGO DELTA

Eagle Island Camp (91.40) Get up close to elephants and kudu by way of a *mokoro* canoe at this remote safari lodge surrounded by water lilies. 800/237-1236; eagleisland camp.com; doubles from $$$$$.

EGYPT

ALEXANDRIA

Four Seasons Hotel Alexandria at San Stefano (87.73) 118 Pierre-Yves Rochon–designed rooms on the Corniche, with Mediterranean views from private balconies and the 4th-floor infinity pool. 399 El Geish Rd.; 800/332-3442; fourseasons.com; doubles from $$.

CAIRO

Four Seasons Hotel Cairo at Nile Plaza (91.77) A 30-story high-rise with 7 restaurants and public spaces that feature contemporary Egyptian art. 1089 Corniche El Nil; 800/332-3442; fourseasons.com; doubles from $$.

Four Seasons Hotel Cairo at the First Residence (91.74) A 269-room glass tower on the Nile—the first Four Seasons in the Middle East— with a view of botanical gardens and the distant Pyramids. 35 Giza St.; 800/332-3442; fourseasons.com; doubles from $$.

❺ **Mena House Oberoi** (89.48) 19th-century lodge with modern wings, a pool complex, and a soon-to-open golf course on 40 acres abutting the Great Pyramid of Khufu. 6 Pyramids Rd.; 800/562-3764; oberoihotels. com; doubles from $–$$.

ISRAEL

JERUSALEM

King David Hotel (88.45) Iconic limestone 1930's landmark near the Old City; updated touches include the 5th and 6th floors (redone by Adam Tihany) and an of-the-moment French restaurant. 23 King David St.; 800/223-7773; danhotels.com; doubles from $$–$$$.

JORDAN

AMMAN

❺ **Four Seasons Hotel** (90.00) Hilltop 15-story limestone-and-glass tower—the top pick of diplomats— between the Sweifiyah shopping area

and the financial district. Al-Kindi St.; 800/332-3442; fourseasons.com; doubles from $, including breakfast.

DEAD SEA

❺ **Kempinski Hotel Ishtar** (91.20) Babylonian-style structure with 345 contemporary rooms and one of the largest spas in the Middle East; treatments include local sea-salt body scrubs and hammam rituals. Swaimeh; 800/426-3135; kempinski. com; doubles from $.

KENYA

AMBOSELI NATIONAL PARK

Tortilis Camp (89.33) The park's only luxe property, facing Mount Kilimanjaro; 17 canvas tents, plus a 2-room family suite (1 double and 2 twin beds and a private veranda). 254-20/600-3090; tortilis.com; doubles from $$$–$$$$$, all-inclusive.

MASAI MARA

&Beyond Kichwa Tembo (92.46) Two camps (one rustic, the other colonial) managed by the outfitter &Beyond, lauded for its conservation efforts to protect the park's rare leopards, honey badgers, and zebras. 888/882-3742; andbeyond.com; doubles from $$–$$$$$, all-inclusive.

Fairmont Mara Safari Club (92.57) 50 luxurious tents on a Mara River oxbow (a hippo-viewing hot spot); a property known for activities including fishing and birding tours. 800/441-1414; fairmont.com; doubles from $$$–$$$$.

Governors' Camp (90.75) A riverside tented village near the Masai Mara's wildebeest migration corridors, with farm-fresh cuisine thanks to deliveries from Nairobi markets. 254-20/273-4000; governorscamp.com; doubles from $$$–$$$$$, including meals.

Mara Serena Safari Lodge (89.56) 74 modern domed huts modeled after a Masai village for unobstructed views of roaming elephants and giraffes. 254-20/284-2000; serenahotels.com; doubles from $$–$$$$$, including meals.

MBIRIKANI GROUP RANCH

Ol Donyo Lodge (97.71) 10 suites with savanna-side infinity pools, outdoor showers, and rooftop

sleeping areas for nighttime views of Mount Kilimanjaro. 866/930-9124; greatplainsconservation.com; doubles from $$$$, all-inclusive.

NAIROBI

Fairmont The Norfolk (87.46) Tudor-style hotel, tropical gardens, and a new teahouse, wine bar, and steak house. A frequent jumping-off point for safaris. Harry Thuku Rd.; 800/441-1414; fairmont.com; doubles from $$.

NANYUKI

Fairmont Mount Kenya Safari Club (95.64) Stylishly updated 1950's-era hunting lodge on 100 acres in the Mount Kenya foothills. 800/441-1414; fairmont.com; doubles from $$$, including meals.

MOROCCO

MARRAKESH

La Mamounia (87.27) Legendary 1923 hotel, gleaming after a 3-year, $180 million renovation, with 4 restaurants (Italian, French, Moroccan, and casual Mediterranean) that use produce from the on-site garden. Ave. Bab Jdid; 212-524/388-600; mamounia. com; doubles from $$$.

SOUTH AFRICA

CAPE TOWN

Cape Grace (92.35) Mansard-roofed 120-room hotel, spa, and yacht, on a private Victoria & Alfred Waterfront quay. West Quay Rd.; 800/223-6800; capegrace.com; doubles from $$$, including breakfast.

Mount Nelson Hotel (91.12) 1899 property with a new South African restaurant (rooibos-cured ostrich; springbok pie) on 9 leafy acres convenient to beaches and Table Mountain. 76 Orange St.; 800/237-1236; mountnelson.co.za; doubles from $$, including breakfast.

One&Only (88.91) A glamorous new arrival for the Victoria & Alfred Waterfront—double-height entry, 131 high-tech rooms (16 face the water), and an outpost of Nobu. Dock Rd.; 866/552-0001; oneandonly resorts.com; doubles from $$$–$$$$.

Table Bay Hotel (88.00) Maritime-themed hotel with a 246-foot, palm-lined drive on the Victoria & Alfred Waterfront. Quay 6; 800/727-9330; suninternational.com; doubles from $$$, including breakfast.

FRANSCHHOEK

Le Quartier Français (93.82) 21 whimsical suites and a Cape Village–style cottage; notable South African chef Margot Janse oversees both on-site restaurants. 800/735-2478; lequartier.co.za; doubles from $$.

JOHANNESBURG

Saxon Boutique Hotel, Villas & Spa (91.54) Stately 53-suite boutique property on 10 acres in tony Sandhurst, where Nelson Mandela stayed for 6 months in the 1990's. 36 Saxon Rd.; 27-11/292-6000; saxon.co.za; doubles from $$$$, including breakfast.

Westcliff Hotel (88.00) Nine coral-pink stone villas (115 rooms in total) set among terraced gardens. Think of it as safari lite, thanks to views of the elephants in the Johannesburg zoo. 67 Jan Smuts Ave.; 800/237-1236; westcliff.co.za; doubles from $$, including breakfast.

KRUGER NATIONAL PARK AREA

Londolozi Private Game Reserve (93.39) Five family-run lodges on 42,000 wilderness acres known for leopard sightings. 27-11/280-6655; londolozi.com; doubles from $$$$$, all-inclusive.

MalaMala Game Reserve (90.20) Trio of camps plus a wine cellar, library, and infinity pool on South Africa's largest private Big Five preserve. 27-11/442-2267; malamala.com; doubles from $$$$$, all-inclusive.

Royal Malewane (97.88) Eight-suite luxury game lodge on 30,000 acres with old-fashioned activities (hot-air-balloon rides; horseback safaris) and a 3-to-1 staff-to-guest ratio. 27-15/793-3977; royalmalewane.com; doubles from $$$$$, all-inclusive.

Sabi Sabi Private Game Reserve–Bush Lodge (91.73) 25 understated thatched-roof suites that spotlight the property's African art collection, plus a new interactive children's center. 804/767-9770; sabisabi.com; doubles from $$$$$, all-inclusive.

Singita Kruger National Park (93.50) Two lodges (1 raised) with

fashionable interiors by African designers, in the Lebombo Mountain range. 27-21/683-6424; singita.com; doubles from $$$$$, all-inclusive.

Singita Sabi Sand (97.95) Three lodges and an impressive wine program. 27-21/683-6424; singita.com; doubles from $$$$$, all-inclusive.

KWAZULU-NATAL

&Beyond Phinda Private Game Reserve (87.20) Six stylish lodges in the 56,000-acre KwaZulu-Natal preserve, near the Sodwana Bay for scuba and fishing excursions. Phinda Game Reserve; 888/882-3742; andbeyond.com; doubles from $$$$–$$$$$, all-inclusive.

TANZANIA

NGORONGORO CRATER

&Beyond Ngorongoro Crater Lodge (95.14) Masai-inspired huts with Victorian touches (Persian carpets; velvet-tufted settees) in 3 camps along the rim of a crater. 888/882-3742; andbeyond.com; doubles from $$$$$, all-inclusive.

Ngorongoro Serena Safari Lodge (89.76) 75-room lodge covered in vines near the Olduvai Gorge—the so-called Cradle of Civilization. 255-27/2537-0505; serenahotels.com; doubles from $$–$$$, including all meals.

Ⓢ **Ngorongoro Sopa Lodge** (87.60) Rondavel-like suites with floor-to-ceiling windows that look out onto a crater frequented by black rhinos. 800/806-9565; sopalodges.com; doubles from $–$$, including meals.

SERENGETI NATIONAL PARK

Kirawira Tented Camp (96.71) Watch the annual wildebeest migration from one of the 25 Victorian-style camps in the western Serengeti. 255-28/2621-5182; serenahotels.com; doubles from $$$–$$$$, including meals.

Serengeti Migration Camp (96.50) 20 tents with wraparound porches and attentive service along the Grumeti River, a popular gathering spot for hippos. 800/806-9565; elewana.com; doubles from $$$$$, all-inclusive.

Serengeti Serena Safari Lodge (88.55) Thatched-roof huts with local Makonde-style carvings among acacia trees in the Serengeti. 255-28/262-

2612; serenahotels.com; doubles from $$–$$$, including meals.

Ⓢ **Serengeti Sopa Lodge** (90.10) Secluded 79-suite hotel with African interiors (traditional masks; handmade wood furnishings), overlooking the plains. 800/806-9565; sopalodges.com; doubles from $–$$, including meals.

Singita Grumeti Reserves (98.44) A luxurious mobile safari is the latest addition to this 340,000-acre concession with 4 separate camps. 27-21/683-6424; singita.com; doubles from $$$$$, all-inclusive.

UNITED ARAB EMIRATES

ABU DHABI

Emirates Palace (92.00) Reportedly the most expensive hotel ever built: 1,002 Swarovski chandeliers, 114 mosaic glass domes, and 394 rooms that feel like palaces. W. Corniche Rd.; 971-2/690-9000; emiratespalace.ae; doubles from $$$$$.

DUBAI

Burj Al Arab (88.97) Sail-shaped icon on its own island in the Arabian Gulf. The 202 bi-level suites start at a massive 1,830 square feet. Jumeirah Beach Rd.; 877/854-8051; jumeirah.com; doubles from $$$$$.

Grand Hyatt (87.77) 674-room complex with 14 restaurants and an indoor rain forest where dhow boats are suspended from the ceiling. Sheikh Rashid Rd.; 800/233-1234; hyatt.com; doubles from $$.

ZAMBIA

LIVINGSTONE

Royal Livingstone (88.29) 173 soon-to-be-updated colonial-style rooms in an estate-like setting close enough to Victoria Falls to be sprinkled by mist. 800/727-9330; suninternational.com; doubles from $$$$.

ASIA

BHUTAN

PARO

Uma Paro (90.93) A 29-room Himalayan retreat and spa that mixes

cozy Bhutanese touches (timber furnishings; traditional wood-burning stoves) with adventure (trekking; biking; photo tours). 975-8/271-597; como.bz; doubles from $$, including breakfast.

CAMBODIA

SIEM REAP

Ⓢ **Hôtel de la Paix** (87.76) This stylishly transformed 1957 Siem Reap landmark has a sugar palm–flanked entrance and a new lobby-side international art gallery. Sivutha Blvd.; 855-63/966-000; hoteldelapaixangkor.com; doubles from $–$$, including breakfast.

Raffles Grand Hotel d'Angkor (89.33) Centrally located grande dame set within a 15-acre French garden just a 15-minute drive from Angkor Wat. 1 Vithei Charles de Gaulle; 800/768-9009; raffles.com; doubles from $$$, including breakfast.

Ⓢ **Sofitel Angkor Phokeethra Golf & Spa Resort** (88.00) A regal retreat (antique ceiling fans; Cambodia's largest swimming pool) on Siem Reap's tranquil periphery. Vithei Charles de Gaulle; 800/763-4835; sofitel.com; doubles from $.

CHINA

BEIJING

Ⓢ **Peninsula Beijing** (87.57) Opulent hotel with one of the city's finest spas, located in the luxury-shopping enclave of Wangfujing. 8 Goldfish Lane; 866/382-8388; peninsula.com; doubles from $–$$.

Ritz-Carlton (89.38) The Ritz's classic Chippendale-and-chintz aesthetic, in Chaoyang bordering the Central Business District. 83A Jian Guo Rd., China Central Place; 800/241-3333; ritzcarlton.com; doubles from $$$$.

Ritz-Carlton Beijing, Financial Street (94.00) Feng shui principles (animal sculptures near doorways; fountains surrounding the hotel) prevail at this glass-and-chrome skyscraper. Business travelers will find the Financial District location convenient. 1 Jin Cheng Fang St. E. at Financial St.; 800/241-3333; ritzcarlton.com; doubles from $$–$$$.

A Deluxe room
with views
of the Himalayas
at Uma Paro,
in Bhutan.

HONG KONG

InterContinental (89.07) 495-room Kowloon hotel with 24-hour butlers, restaurants by Alain Ducasse and Nobu Matsuhisa, and dazzling Victoria Harbour views. 18 Salisbury Rd.; 800/327-0200; ichotelsgroup.com; doubles from $$–$$$.

Island Shangri-La (89.57) Soaring skyscraper with 565 mahogany- and crystal-chandelier-appointed rooms, above the tony Pacific Place Mall. Pacific Place, Supreme Court Rd.; 866/565-5050; shangri-la.com; doubles from $$$–$$$$.

Mandarin Oriental (91.02) Graciously updated 1960's-era mid-rise hotel (plus a 3-floor spa and 10 restaurants and bars), at the heart of bustling Central Hong Kong. 5 Connaught Rd.; 800/526-6566; mandarinoriental.com; doubles from $$$–$$$$.

Peninsula Hong Kong (90.70) This 1928 Kowloon landmark (with a Philippe Starck–designed restaurant) will begin a phased overhaul of all 300 guest rooms this year. Salisbury Rd.; 866/382-8388; peninsula.com; doubles from $$$.

Ritz-Carlton (88.00) The new 312-room property is the world's highest hotel, rising 118 floors above Kowloon.

International Commerce Centre, 1 Austin Rd. W.; 800/241-3333; ritzcarlton.com; doubles from $$$–$$$$.

SHANGHAI

Four Seasons Hotel (87.38) 422-room, 37-story luxury tower 1 block from Nanjing Road shopping, with a grand lobby (featuring nightly live piano music) and excellent business amenities. 500 Weihai Rd.; 800/332-3442; fourseasons.com; doubles from $$.

Ⓢ **Hyatt on the Bund** (87.16) Two-tower skyscraper with views of the nearby Huangpu River (check it out from the 31st-floor Vue bar) and 4 restaurants, one serving melt-in-your-mouth Peking duck. 199 Huangpu Rd.; 800/233-1234; hyatt.com; doubles from $–$$.

Park Hyatt (87.73) 174 Tony Chi-designed minimalist luxury rooms on floors 79–93 of the Shanghai World Financial Center. 100 Century Ave.; 877/875-4658; park.hyatt.com; doubles from $$–$$$$.

Portman Ritz-Carlton (87.68) 610-room 1998 monolith that set an early standard for Shanghai luxury, with recently renovated rooms and lobby

areas, plus a dedicated technology butler. 1376 Nanjing Xi Rd.; 800/241-3333; ritzcarlton.com; doubles from $$$.

Pudong Shangri-La (87.27) Top-notch amenities (Adam Tihany–designed restaurant; on-site shopping; a Himalayan-themed spa) and riverfront views in Pudong's Lujiazui financial district. 33 Fu Cheng Rd.; 866/565-5050; shangri-la.com; doubles from $$.

Ⓢ **Westin Bund Center** (87.86) Two streamlined towers, a stylish lobby, and a Banyan Tree Spa, just a 5-minute walk from the historic Bund. 88 Henan Central Rd.; 800/228-3000; westin.com; doubles from $–$$.

INDIA

AGRA

ITC Mughal, a Luxury Collection Hotel (87.77) Princely 35-acre icon made up of ornate mini palaces, 2½ miles outside the city. A new wing added 42 rooms with plunge pools. Taj Ganj; 800/325-3589; ichotels.in; doubles from $$, including breakfast.

Oberoi Amarvilas (95.33) Moghul-themed 102-room palace mirroring the nearby Taj Mahal—all Moorish archways, intricate pavilions, and fountained courtyards. Taj E. Gate Rd.; 800/562-3764; oberoihotels.com; doubles from $$$–$$$$.

JAIPUR

Oberoi Rajvilas (96.92) Channel your inner maharajah at this majestic 32-acre countryside resort made up of tents and villas and a traditional Indian spa. Goner Rd.; 800/562-3764; oberoihotels.com; doubles from $$$–$$$$.

Rambagh Palace (92.34) 19th-century hunting lodge turned opulent palace hotel (carved pillars; mirror-and-stone embellishments) among manicured gardens. Bhawani Singh Rd.; 866/969-1825; tajhotels.com; doubles from $$$.

JODHPUR

Umaid Bhawan Palace (92.24) Once the largest private residence in the world, now a 347-room sandstone Taj palace hotel with daily champagne art tours to see the antiques and 105-foot cupola. 866/969-1825; tajhotels.com; doubles from $$$$, including breakfast.

KOCHI

Vivanta by Taj-Malabar (87.73) 96-room South Indian escape by Taj's new relaxed resort brand, on an island just half a mile from Cochin Harbor. Willingdon Island; 866/969-1825; tajhotels.com; doubles from $$.

MUMBAI

The Oberoi (91.27) Recently renovated 287-room flagship above the Queen's Necklace. Unusual extras: a cherry-red grand piano and a 24-hour spa. Nariman Point; 800/562-3764; oberoihotels.com; doubles from $$.

Taj Mahal Palace (92.42) 1903 emblem of Raj-era Bombay—still the city's grande dame—overlooking the Gateway of India. Apollo Bunder; 866/969-1825; tajhotels.com; doubles from $$, including breakfast.

NEW DELHI

Ⓢ **The Imperial** (91.77) Art Deco icon—now with a state-of-the-art salon and spa, plus India's only Chanel boutique—steps from Connaught Place. Janpath; 91-11/2334-1234; theimperialindia.com; doubles from $–$$.

The Oberoi (90.59) Graceful, business-friendly hotel close to Humayun's Tomb and Khan Market, with superb on-site restaurants and bars (from dim sum to a wine cellar) and an adjacent golf course. Dr. Zakir Hussain Marg; 800/562-3764; oberoihotels.com; doubles from $$.

Ⓢ **Taj Mahal Hotel** (91.50) 11-story landmark close to the city's diplomatic and political heart; its butlers and astrologers are favored by New Delhi's power players. 1 Mansingh Rd.; 866/969-1825; tajhotels.com; doubles from $–$$.

Taj Palace Hotel (88.91) 402-room behemoth, 10 minutes from the city center, with staffer-led excursions to galleries and spice markets. Sardar Patel Marg, Diplomatic Enclave; 866/969-1825; tajhotels.com; doubles from $$, including breakfast and airport transfers.

UDAIPUR

Oberoi Udaivilas (97.70) A 30-acre Mewari-style palace on the banks of Lake Pichola, complete with private motorboats, a traditional Kashmiri gondola, and sprawling courtyards rimmed by reflecting pools. Haridasji ki Magri; 800/562-3764; oberoihotels.com; doubles from $$$–$$$$.

Taj Lake Palace (93.43) Centuries-old white-marble palace (intricate silks; frescoed arches) rising from a jagged rock formation in Lake Pichola. 866/969-1825; tajhotels.com; doubles from $$$, including breakfast.

INDONESIA

BALI

Amandari (89.87) Reimagined Balinese village on the outskirts of Ubud, with stellar cultural programs thanks to long-standing community connections. Kedewatan, Ubud; 800/477-9180; amanresorts.com; doubles from $$$$.

JAPAN

KYOTO

Hyatt Regency (87.67) Traditional touches (kimono-covered headboards; *washi*-paper lampshades) plus interiors by Super Potato, in Higashiyama Shichijo. 644-2 Sanju-sangendo-mawari; 800/233-1234; hyatt.com; doubles from $$–$$$.

TOKYO

Grand Hyatt (88.67) Polished 387-room hotel—centrally located in Roppongi Hills—with 7 in-house restaurants. 6-10-3 Roppongi; 800/233-1234; hyatt.com; doubles from $$–$$$.

Mandarin Oriental (93.33) 178 spacious guest rooms on select floors of a 38-story skyscraper that towers over the Nihonbashi district. 2-1-1 Nihonbashi Muromachi, Chuo-ku; 800/526-6566; mandarinoriental.com; doubles from $$$–$$$$.

Park Hyatt (88.78) 178-room urban oasis in Shinjuku, featured in Sofia Coppola's *Lost in Translation*. 3-7-1-2 Nishi-Shinjuku; 877/875-4658; park.hyatt.com; doubles from $$$–$$$$.

Peninsula Tokyo (92.24) 314-room hotel—the reigning queen of the city's new guard—facing the Imperial Palace Gardens and Hibiya Park; expert concierge service sets it apart. 1-8-1 Yuraku-cho, Chiyoda-ku; 866/382-8388; peninsula.com; doubles from $$$$.

LAOS

LUANG PRABANG

La Résidence Phou Vao (95.20) French-colonial, all-suite wellness retreat on a frangipani-dotted hill above Luang Prabang; the first Laotian property to use only local ingredients for traditional spa treatments. 800/237-1236; residence phouvao.com; doubles from $$$.

MALAYSIA

KUALA LUMPUR

⑤ Mandarin Oriental (90.95) 30-story building offering panoramic views of the Petronas Twin Towers. The newly added pan-Asian restaurant Mosaic overlooks the City Center Park. Kuala Lumpur City Center; 800/526-6566; mandarinoriental.com; doubles from $, including breakfast.

⑤ Ritz-Carlton (90.80) Modern, 250-room hotel that dominates the Golden Triangle district, preferred by business travelers. 168 Jalan Imbi; 800/241-3333; ritzcarlton.com; doubles from $–$$.

PERAK

⑤ Pangkor Laut Resort (90.00) 43 overwater villas on a private isle off the western coast of Malaysia— a lush, undiscovered hideaway. 603/2783-1000; pangkorlautresort. com; doubles from $–$$, including breakfast.

PHILIPPINES

BORACAY ISLAND

Discovery Shores (92.93) 88 suites on a tiny island known for powdery white sand; butlers keep beachgoers supplied with ice-cold drinks. 63-36/288-4500; discovery shoresboracay.com; doubles from $$, including breakfast.

MANILA

Makati Shangri-La (91.56) The spot for power players: a 699-room curvilinear skyscraper overlooking the financial district. Ayala and Makati Aves.; 866/565-5050; shangri-la.com; doubles from $$.

Peninsula Manila (90.86) A pair of historic 11-story towers rising above a lavish restored lobby in Manila's financial hub. 1226 Makati City; 866/382-8388; peninsula.com; doubles from $$.

SINGAPORE

⑤ Fairmont (88.00) A 769-room, I. M. Pei-designed tower in the Bras Basah arts district; the spa is one of Asia's largest. 80 Bras Basah Rd.; 800/441-1414; fairmont.com; doubles from $–$$.

Four Seasons Hotel (89.50) One of the city's more intimate properties, with 225 rooms (chinoiserie; tufted leather headboards; high ceilings), dim sum, and views of Orchard Boulevard's boutiques. 190 Orchard Blvd.; 800/332-3442; fourseasons. com; doubles from $$.

Mandarin Oriental (91.48) Behind a fan-shaped façade near Marina Square. At Melt restaurant, 30 chefs whip up Japanese, pan-Asian, and international dishes at cooking stations. Raffles Ave.; 800/526-6566; mandarinoriental.com; doubles from $$–$$$.

Marina Bay Sands (87.82) Moshe Safdie's gargantuan 2,651-room fantasy, with restaurants by luminaries such as Daniel Boulud and Guy Savoy, and the cantilevered SkyPark, where the world's largest outdoor infinity pool resides. 10 Bayfront Ave.; 866/263-4598; marina baysands.com; doubles from $$.

Raffles Hotel (89.06) 103 colonial-style suites in cloister-like buildings with breezy verandas; the fabled property that once welcomed Noël Coward and Somerset Maugham. 1 Beach Rd.; 800/768-9009; raffles. com; doubles from $$$$.

St. Regis (92.23) A downtown high-rise with 24-hour butler service, a fleet of Bentleys, plus unique amenities (defogging mirrors; an Enomatic wine-serving system) and one of Asia's best private art collections. 29 Tanglin Rd.; 877/787-3447; stregis.com; doubles from $$$$, including breakfast.

SOUTH KOREA

SEOUL

Grand Hyatt (89.65) 18 acres of waterfalls and landscaped gardens— plus 601 rooms—overlooking the Han River or Mount Namsan. 322 Sowol-ro, Yongsan-gu; 800/233-1234; hyatt.com; doubles from $$.

THAILAND

BANGKOK

⑤ Banyan Tree (89.00) All-suite skyscraper that's also home to a signature spa and the popular 61st-floor Vertigo Grill & Moon Bar. 21/100 S. Sathon Rd.; 800/591-0439; banyantree.com; doubles from $.

A Cottage suite at New Zealand's Huka Lodge.

Four Seasons Hotel (89.37)
Timeless Asian oasis (gardens; hand-painted silks) with a renovated pearl-gray-and-turquoise lobby and 2 spa suites with private plunge pools and steam rooms. 155 Rajadamri Rd.; 800/332-3442; fourseasons.com; doubles from $$.

⑤ Grand Hyatt Erawan (88.00)
Ultramodern retreat that overlooks the Erawan Shrine. The 75,000-square-foot, Tony Chi–designed spa offers fitness classes and personal training. 494 Rajadamri Rd.; 800/233-1234; hyatt.com; doubles from $–$$.

JW Marriott Hotel (88.00)
Black marble high-rise right on Bangkok's main shopping drag, with a cooking school, an American-style steak house, and a bakery. Soi 2, 4 Sukhumvit Rd.; 800/228-9290; jwmarriott.com; doubles from $$.

⑤ Le Méridien (88.24) The 2007-relaunched flagship has platform beds, lacquered-wood bathrooms, and high-tech amenities. A partnership with a nearby design center means impressive in-room art. 40/5 Surawong Rd.; 800/543-4300; lemeridien.com; doubles from $.

Mandarin Oriental (94.49)
135-year-old landmark on the Chao Phraya River with a rich literary history, butler service, and 9 restaurants. 48 Oriental Ave.; 800/526-6566; mandarinoriental.com; doubles from $$.

Peninsula Bangkok (93.49)
37-story tower with 370 rooms, a 3-story spa, and top dining, at the river's edge in Thonburi; complimentary water taxis shuttle guests to the Skytrain. 333 Charoennakorn Rd.; 866/382-8388; peninsula.com; doubles from $$.

⑤ Royal Orchid Sheraton Hotel & Towers (89.76) Recently renovated 726-room hotel and new open-air restaurant and bar in the commercial district, a short boat ride from the Grand Palace. Soi 30, 2 Charoen Krung Rd.; 800/325-3535; sheraton.com; doubles from $.

Shangri-La Hotel (90.77) An 802-room riverfront Bangrak district tower fresh off a $60 million renovation; the

new solar-panel water-heating system is the largest ever installed in a Bangkok hotel. Soi 89, Wat Suan Plu New Rd.; 866/565-5050; shangri-la.com; doubles from $$.

⑤ Sheraton Grande Sukhumvit, a Luxury Collection Hotel (88.19)
Central 420-room property close to the Skytrain; the weekend BarSu music performances draw a crowd. 250 Sukhumvit Rd.; 800/325-3589; sheratongrandesukhumvit.com; doubles from $.

The Sukhothai (88.25) 210 updated rooms in pavilions set amid lotus ponds completes the scene at Bangkok's most peaceful urban retreat. 13/3 S. Sathorn Rd.; 66-23/448-888; sukhothai.com; doubles from $$.

CHIANG MAI

Four Seasons Resort (93.14)
Tranquil refuge on terraced rice paddies outside the northern Thai city, with haute-rustic rooms set in teak pavilions, pool houses, and outdoor relaxation areas. Cooking classes are well-regarded. Mae Rim-Samoeng Old Rd.; 800/332-3442; fourseasons.com; doubles from $$$.

Mandarin Oriental Dhara Dhevi (97.00) A miniature Thai kingdom with 123 Lanna-inspired suites and villas on 60 acres that's the setting for a Buddhist prayer site, a 33,000-square-foot spa, and an arts-and-crafts village. 51/4 Chiang Mai-Sankampaeng Rd.; 800/526-6566; mandarinoriental.com; doubles from $$$.

CHIANG RAI

Anantara Golden Triangle Resort & Spa (89.71) 19 thatched-roof suites amid rolling hills along the Mekong River, where Thailand, Burma, and Laos meet. The hotel's conservation center welcomed the birth of a baby elephant last year. Chiang Saen; 66-53/784-084; anantara.com; doubles from $$$$$, all-inclusive.

PHUKET

⑤ Dusit Thani Laguna Resort (91.47) Activity-filled resort in the Laguna Phuket complex; the place for *muay thai* kickboxing lessons and sailing along Bang Tao Beach. Talang; 66-76/362-999; dusit.com; doubles from $–$$$.

⑤ JW Marriott Phuket Resort & Spa (89.60) Secluded eco-resort and spa beside a pristine stretch of Mai Khao beach. Talang; 800/228-9290; jwmarriott.com; doubles from $–$$.

VIETNAM

HANOI

⑤ Sofitel Legend Metropole (93.51) The city's old-world hideaway. A $20 million redo added a 7-story tower, a spa, and Angelina restaurant; rooms in the original wing maintain a traditional feel. 15 Ngo Quyen St.; 800/763-4835; sofitel.com; doubles from $–$$.

HO CHI MINH CITY

Park Hyatt Saigon (91.74) Colonial meets contemporary on the main square, with a pair of top-notch restaurants and 2 Lam Son, the city's only nonsmoking bar. 2 Lam Son Square, District 1; 877/875-4568; park.hyatt.com; doubles from $$.

AUSTRALIA, NEW ZEALAND + THE SOUTH PACIFIC

AUSTRALIA

KATOOMBA

Lilianfels Blue Mountain Resort & Spa (89.87) 85-room storybook country manor in the Blue Mountains, just 90 minutes from Sydney. 61-2/4780-1200; lilianfels.com.au; doubles from $$–$$$.

MELBOURNE

Langham Hotel (90.55) Langham's first hotel down under, located between the Royal Botanic Gardens and the Yarra River, now with Club Terrace rooms that open onto 527-square-foot balconies. 1 Southgate Ave.; 800/588-9141; langhamhotels.com; doubles from $$–$$$.

Park Hyatt (90.29) Peaceful Art Deco gem overlooking St. Patrick's Cathedral, a 5-minute stroll from downtown. 1 Parliament Square; 877/875-4658; park.hyatt.com; doubles from $$–$$$.

SYDNEY

InterContinental (88.53) Centrally located tower set in the 1851 Treasury Building; the Club InterContinental lounge has some of the best harbor views in town. 117 Macquarie St.; 800/327-0200; intercontinental.com; doubles from $$.

Park Hyatt (88.00) Four-story hotel, primed after a $65 million transformation, that's now topped by 3 new rooftop suites—directly opposite the Opera House. 7 Hickson Rd.; 877/875-4658; park.hyatt.com; doubles from $$$$.

FRENCH POLYNESIA

BORA-BORA

InterContinental Bora Bora Resort & Thalasso Spa (93.56)
The ultimate fantasy: 80 Polynesian-style villas perched above an azure lagoon along the Motu Piti Aau coral reef. 800/327-0200; intercontinental.com; doubles from $$$$$.

NEW ZEALAND

MATAURI BAY

Lodge at Kauri Cliffs (96.25)
North Island cliffside lodge, golf course, and top spa on 6,000 acres with waterfalls and private beaches. 800/735-2478; kauricliffs.com; doubles from $$$$$, including breakfast and dinner.

QUEENSTOWN

Sofitel Queenstown Hotel & Spa (87.33) French-style, 82-room hotel and new lobby on the edge of Queenstown's lively center, reborn after a $2 million upgrade in 2011. 800/763-4835; sofitel.com; doubles from $$–$$$.

TAUPO

Huka Lodge (92.57) The ne plus ultra of New Zealand lodges, thanks to an idyllic Waikato River garden setting and an extensive roster of activities (fishing, hiking, golf). 64-7/378-5791; hukalodge.com; doubles from $$$$$, including breakfast and dinner.

A peaceful spot
at GoldenEye
Hotel & Resort,
in Jamaica.

TRIPS DIRECTORY

A foldaway desk at
25hours Hotel
HafenCity, in Hamburg,
Germany.

INDEX

A suite at the Redbury, in Los Angeles.

CONTRIBUTORS

Christine Ajudua

Richard Alleman

Nicole Alper

Tom Austin

Aimee Lee Ball

J.D. Banks

Colin Barraclough

Kate Betts

Vinita Bharadwaj

Laura Begley Bloom

Dominique Browning

Aric Chen

Jennifer Chen

Tanvi Chheda

Christine Ciarmello

Colleen Clark

Anthony Dennis

Stephen Drucker

Mark Ellwood

Hui Fang

Amy Farley

Erin Florio

Jennifer Flowers

Peter J. Frank

Eleni N. Gage

Michael Gross

Margot Guralnick

Sue Henly

Farhad Heydari

Catesby Holmes

Karrie Jacobs

David Kaufman

David A. Keeps

Stirling Kelso

Sarah Khan

Christopher Kucway

Sandy Lang

Matt and Ted Lee

Peter Jon Lindberg

Heather Smith MacIsaac

Charles Maclean

Alexandra Marshall

Ralph Martin

Mario R. Mercado

Alison Miller

Elizabeth Minchilli

Heidi Mitchell

Shane Mitchell

Niloufar Motamed

Shira Nanus

Lindsey Olander

Kathryn O'Shea-Evans

Douglas Rogers

Julian Rubinstein

Adam Sachs

Antonella Salem

Bruce Schoenfeld

Kristina Schreck

Dani Shapiro

Jim Shi

Maria Shollenbarger

Paola Singer

Sarah Spagnolo

Valerie Stivers-Isakova

Ed Stocker

Rima Suqi

Laura Teusink

Guy Trebay

Shivani Vora

Valerie Waterhouse

Stephen Whitlock

Ingrid K. Williams

Posing in front of
the entrance
mural at St. Lucia's
Hotel Chocolat.

PHOTOGRAPHERS

Twin perches overlooking the Atlantic Ocean at Kenoa, in Barra de São Miguel, Brazil.